PROMISING
AGAIN

This series examines crucial times in family life in light of the family as a social unit. Individual books address major changes that ordinarily occur in the life cycle of a family and the major tasks of the family: rituals that enable effective transitions as those tasks change; beliefs and values from the Christian tradition that shape and are shaped by those family tasks; and pastoral opportunities in response to family life-cycle agendas. Each volume takes into account family systems theory and social and economic factors that affect the family.

FAMILY LIVING
IN PASTORAL PERSPECTIVE

LEAVING HOME
Herbert Anderson and Kenneth R. Mitchell

BECOMING MARRIED
Herbert Anderson and Robert Cotton Fite

REGARDING CHILDREN
Herbert Anderson and Susan B. W. Johnson

PROMISING AGAIN
Herbert Anderson, David Hogue,
and Marie McCarthy, S.P.

FAMILY LIVING IN PASTORAL PERSPECTIVE

PROMISING
AGAIN

HERBERT ANDERSON
DAVID HOGUE
AND MARIE MCCARTHY, S.P.

WESTMINSTER JOHN KNOX PRESS
LOUISVILLE, KENTUCKY

To Phyllis, Diane, and the Sisters of Providence with whom we each promise again and again.

© 1995 Herbert Anderson, David Hogue, and Marie McCarthy, S.P.

Scripture quotations from the New Revised Standard Version of the Bible are copyright © 1989 by the Division of Christian Education of the National Council of the Churches of Christ in the U.S.A. and are used by permission.

Excerpt from "Little Gidding" in FOUR QUARTETS, copyright 1943 by T. S. Eliot and renewed 1971 by Esme Valerie Eliot, reprinted by permission of Harcourt, Brace & Company.

Book design by Drew Stevens
Cover design by Jeff Tull, Fearless Designs

First edition

Published by Westminster John Knox Press
Louisville, Kentucky

This book is printed on acid-free paper that meets the American National Standards Institute Z39.48 standard. ♾

PRINTED IN THE UNITED STATES OF AMERICA

95 96 97 98 99 00 01 02 03 04 — 10 9 8 7 6 5 4 3 2 1

Library of Congress Cataloging-in-Publication Data

Anderson, Herbert, 1936-
    Promising again / Herbert Anderson, David Hogue, Marie McCarthy, S.P.
  - 1st ed.
        p.   cm. — (Family living in pastoral perspective 4th bk.)
      ISBN 0-664-25124-2 (alk. paper)
      1. Life change events—Religious aspects—Christianity.   2. Pastoral counseling.
  3. Adjustment (Psychology)   I. Hogue, David.   II. McCarthy, Marie, S.P. 1942-
  III. Title.   IV. Series: Anderson, Herbert, 1936-   Family living in pastoral
  perspective; 4th bk.
  BV4509.5.A52   1995
  248.8′44—dc20   95-35443

CONTENTS

ILLUSTRATIONS

INTRODUCTION

OUR SECOND and last child graduated from high school just before we moved to Chicago. Phyllis had already begun working and living in Chicago and loved the challenge of her new job. Because I was not teaching that summer, I met neighbors, located stores, and found a dentist and a dependable auto mechanic. I was less confident, however, about hanging pictures. It took a while for us to make our townhouse a home. When we returned home at the end of the summer, having taken our daughter to college, the nest was emptier. We now needed to make the transition from being a couple with children to one without children again.

During the summer, we began a pattern of role reversal in the marriage that still continues today. I had decided—somewhat unilaterally—that because my schedule was more flexible, I would assume the majority of the household responsibilities. I liked cooking, although I did not like cleaning toilets. My conscious reason for initiating this change was to make it easier for Phyllis and give us more time together when she was home. However, it also gave me an identity and a distraction that allowed me to temporarily avoid the intimidating factor of living and teaching in the shadow of the University of Chicago.

For us, this ordinary task in our family's life was complicated by the fact that we were in a new home and in a new city, with changing roles and demanding jobs. We also had different expectations of this new phase of our life together. Now that the children were launched, Phyllis looked forward to the freedom of investing fully in her work without worrying that she was neglecting our children. By contrast, I had visions of a more relaxed life without the obligations of parenting.

1

My household plan backfired. Because Phyllis was more needed at work than at home, she worked longer hours. For a variety of reasons, the discontinuities in our lives at that time were greater than the continuities. It was a bumpy transition.

My saga is similar to the story that every couple could tell about this time of transition in marriage, and yet each situation is unique. Couples who have worked hard to nurture the marital bond during childrearing are still surprised by how much things change when the children leave home. This ordinary moment is complicated if parents are reluctant to launch their children or children are reluctant to leave. Responsibility for elderly parents also may make a time of transition into a stressful crisis. Launching children is an ordinary time of change that is complicated by circumstances unique to every couple—the role of their children in the family, the history of the marriage, and their social context. What is common in each situation is the need to promise again. Although we begin with the moment in the life cycle of a family when children are launched, *the purpose of this book is to develop promising again as a metaphor for sustaining and strengthening marriage at any time in its history.*

> Promising again is an intentional, mutual renewal of the marriage covenant whenever major change occurs. It is *intentional* and *mutual* because it requires that both partners actively choose again for the marriage and for each other. It is an act of will. Promising again is a *renewal* because it promotes new life in the marital bond. Because marriage is a dynamic *covenant* rather than a static contract, it is always changing. Promising again occurs at times of expected and unexpected *crisis* when the ordinary ways of being together no longer work.

Marriage as a Pilgrimage of Promising

Marriage means many things. It is a social institution that provides for the care of children, regulates sexual intimacy, and fosters affectional bonds between women and men. It is also a legal institution protected by law and an economic unit of consumption and production. As a sacramental reality, marriage is a gift and a sign undergirded by the promise of God's grace and the sustaining love of a faith community. The marriage relationship is, above all else, covenantal in nature and based on the willingness to hold one's partner in abiding seriousness.

At the core of this marital covenant is an ethic of promising. In a public ceremony, two people promise to love, honor, and cherish each other until death parts them. Marriage is understood as a religious covenant because we believe God is present to sustain this union with grace and love. Nonetheless, marriage is long on possibilities and short on guarantees. When two people promise to love and honor each other until death parts them, they cannot anticipate all the changes that will complicate or challenge the love they profess. Even if the marriage begins with a carefully written prenuptial contract that anticipates the possibility of failure, most couples expect to keep for a lifetime the promises they make to each other on their wedding day. The wedding is a moment for passionate commitments and a high resolve to keep the promises we make.

Episcopal priest John H. Snow has added to our understanding of marriage from a Christian perspective in a way that recognizes the need to promise again. Marriage is a pilgrimage. According to Snow, marriage is a "pilgrimage of promising" sustained by courage and self-giving love. The pilgrim marriage "does not strain to remain the same, but is open and responsive to new people and events which must be met as the couple moves not so much through time as with it, [while] understanding the episodic nature of time, its discrete beginnings and ends and new beginnings."[1] Because a pilgrim marriage recognizes the inevitability of change and the finitude of death, it is characterized by unending beginnings and endings. The gift of another who promises again and again in marriage is an unending occasion for gratitude.

We are using *promising again* instead of *keeping promises* as a central metaphor for family living to acknowledge this dynamic, ever-changing pilgrim character of life and marriage. Change has occurred and will continue to occur in family living as in all other aspects of life. The need to promise again does not always arise because we have failed to keep a promise or a commitment or we have been unfaithful in some way. Rather, promising again is necessary when keeping promises is not enough. We have changed or the situation has changed and we need to renew our promises in the light of those changes.

This book primarily concerns the changes that occur in a marriage because children are leaving home. There are, however, three ordinary moments of significant transition in the history of a marriage: when children are added, when children are launched, and when the couple retires from work outside the home. At those moments, the marital bond is often unsteady enough that couples must reconsider their relationship in order to recommit to one another. *Couples ordinarily need to promise again in order to remain married in a vital way.*

There are extraordinary or unexpected changes in the lives of individuals and families as a whole that also necessitate recommitting to one another. Judith Wallerstein has observed that "because people and life circumstances change over time, marriage is always a work in progress."[2] Some of those changes generate more discontinuity or chaos than the couple can cope with and the marriage ends. *Whenever there is a change significant enough to alter role definition, ritual patterns of interaction, or balance of power in the relationship, wives and husbands need to look for ways to promise again.* We make promises for the sake of stability in marriage. We promise again when change makes recommitment necessary for the sake of fidelity. The paradoxical truth of being married is that couples need to keep changing and promising again in order to maintain a stable bond.

The Aim of the Book

We hope this book will be read by a variety of audiences. It is for parents when adult children are being launched, for couples without children whose occasions for promising again are less predictable, and for those who have been divorced or widowed and are thinking about or planning to marry again. We hope this book will also be helpful for couples when unexpected changes in their lives together create a crisis in the marriage. This practice of promising again also applies for women and men who have vowed to live in religious communities. We intend for pastoral ministers and caring friends to find help in these pages for the task of assisting couples to promise again when a marriage flounders.

We have written this book during a time in which there is increasing public debate about the needs of children and the future of the family. Some say marriage is in decay. The frequency of divorce, postponing marriage to later in life, choosing not to marry at all, or the increasing number of unwed parents are factors that are interpreted as signs of decline. Others say we need to direct our attention to rebuilding a family culture based on enduring marital relationships.[3] Our concern is particularly with understanding what enables marriages to endure.

In her book, *The Good Marriage,* Judith Wallerstein has identified nine tasks that women and men must address and achieve together if a marriage is to succeed. The first two tasks, separating from the home of one's origin and forging a bond of intimacy, are principal themes in the second book in this series, *Becoming Married*. The third task, embracing the daunting role of parenting, is the focus of *Regarding Children*. Wallerstein describes the fourth task of marriage in this way: "to confront and master the inevitable crises of life, maintaining the strength of the bond in the face of adversity."[4] This fourth task is more varied than the others because each crisis evokes different anxieties. Each crisis has the potential to strengthen a marriage, weaken it, or bring it down altogether. This book is a development of this fourth task. *Promising Again* concerns the ongoing recommitment necessary if marriages are to endure, since people and life circumstances keep changing over time.

Staying married is important. With that we concur. Yet two themes are missing in much of the family debate. The first is a recognition that it is not easy to stay married. There are as many cultural trends and demands from the free-market economy that make it difficult to remain married as there are forces that make it easy to divorce or not marry at all. The task of restoring marriage will require fundamental shifts in the attitude of the larger culture. The second concerns providing concrete and practical ways of enhancing marriage, a theme often missing from the current debate. It is often easier to admonish people to reclaim the ideal of marital permanence than to suggest how that restoration might occur. The aim of this book is to provide a new way of thinking about being married that acknowledges the inevitability of change and takes into account those changes as we promise again. We hope not only that the reader will find in this book an empathic approach to the struggles of being married today, but also concrete help for the work of promising again. In the end, however, we believe that marriages endure when the change is deep enough to transform the institution itself and the people in it.

There are many reasons that this book is needed today. Not so long ago, promising again was less necessary because one parent would likely be deceased by the time the last child was ready to leave home. Now, because people live longer and have fewer children, couples are likely to spend more years as middle-aged and older adults in a so-called empty nest. Geographic mobility, distance from one's extended family, economic stress, job inflexibility, the anonymity of urban living, and changing gender expectations add to the likelihood that couples will experience some kind of crisis that makes renewal of the marital bond necessary in order to maintain it. The original wedding promise is not enough to sustain sixty years of marriage. Nor is it realistic to expect that we can keep that promise for a lifetime.

We need a new way of thinking about being married, somewhere between absolutizing the initial promise at the expense of the well-being of individuals *and* absolutizing personal preference or self-realization at the cost of the marital bond. Insisting on keeping a marriage vow may create misery for family members; it also erodes the meaning of marriage itself. The shift from a sacramental view of marriage to a more contractual one has also undermined its significance. As a result, the institution of marriage, as we have come to understand it today, is not always strong enough to sustain the fragile love of a husband and wife. Moreover, it is not easy to remain married when everyone wants to exercise their freedom to pursue personal or professional dreams, or both. We understand promising again as a way of thinking about being married that honors *both* the growth of individuals and the needs of the marital bond.

Each of the partners for this volume comes to the writing task with a different experiential framework. I celebrated my thirtieth wedding anniversary while this volume was being written. David Hogue has been divorced and is now married to a woman who herself has been married before. And Marie McCarthy, S.P., who has never married, continues to promise again and again to her religious community as she celebrates thirty-five years as a Sister of Providence. Each perspective adds a richness to our understanding of the multifaceted process of promising again. All of us, however, regard promising as a fundamental quality of being human that is also essential for living together in community.

Locating This Book in the Series

In the first book in this series, *Leaving Home,* the focus was primarily on the work that must be done by sons and daughters who were separating emotionally from their homes of origin. When parents are willing to let their children go with a blessing, it is easier for adult sons and daughters to leave. In this volume, however, the focus shifts to the work parents must do when children leave. What is at stake in this moment of a family's life cycle is more than the differentiation of children: it is the vitality of marriage itself. Although families are more likely to thrive when promising has been constant throughout the life cycle, it is especially necessary during this time when children are leaving home and being launched.

In the second book, *Becoming Married,* we proposed that bonding in marriage happens over time. The wedding is a public declaration that two people intend to commit themselves to the process of forming a marital bond. Because becoming married is often determined by a series of unnoticed commitments and recommitments that continue over a lifetime, the distinction between becoming married and promising again is an arbitrary one. Moreover, it varies greatly when two people will acknowledge that they are finally married. Promising again, however, presumes that such a primary bond has already been formed. In that sense, promising again begins when becoming married ends.

In the third book in this series, *Regarding Children,* we observed that a marriage is profoundly changed by the addition of children. The change that children bring to a family is an invitation to experience the mystery of life in everyday events of care. Children reveal vulnerabilities and neediness common to us all. When we let them, they expand our vision of what it means to be human. Children also limit our freedom, alter our self-understanding, and catalyze our hopes. The capacity of a couple to adapt to the changes that children necessitate is a sign of the health of their relationship. It is also a prelude to the renewal of their marital bond when the children leave. Those who have developed patterns of parenting that still allow time to nourish the marital bond find it easier to promise again when adult children are launched.

This book originally was to be titled *Marrying Again.* Too many people, when they first heard the title, linked it with second marriages. *Promising Again* is a more inclusive title that we will use in three different ways: recommitment when children are being launched; renegotiation of the marital bond between the wedding and the time of launching children whenever there is a change that is significant enough to destabilize the system; and remarriage after death or divorce. Although promising again is a metaphor with many meanings in different contexts, we hope that it will provide a way of reframing what is necessary to make and keep marriages vital.

The themes of promising and promising again are developed in the first chapter from both psychological and theological perspectives. In chapter 2, we examine the need for promising again when the nest is emptying as children leave home. Chapter 3 includes a discussion of several extraordinary moments in the history of a family in which changes are discontinuous enough to warrant reconsidering and renew-

7

ing the marital bond in order to maintain it. In chapter 4, we will explore ways in which the metaphor of promising again might be useful for ministering with couples when the marriage is floundering. The focus of chapter 5 is on marrying again after death or divorce. In the concluding chapter, we explore the need for transformation in marriage that moves beyond adaptation in order to deepen the promises we continue to make.

Looking at Family from a Life-Cycle Perspective

As shown in figure 1, each of the five volumes in this series, Family Living in Pastoral Perspective, examines one of the changes that can be expected in the ordinary life cycle of a family: leaving home, becoming married, raising children, promising again, and living alone. The particular, intimate, often conflicted human crucible that we call the family begins to shape us even before birth. Our families hand us a legacy—their sense of what is right and wrong, their rituals, their peculiar rules—all with the same sense that these are not peculiar at all, but the universal rules by which human beings live. It is often a shock to discover that our family's way is only one of many ways, and that the way we thought was universal might not even be the best way. The legacy we have received from our families of origin is the first and most powerful resource we have to help us negotiate the transitions and changes that mark our family's history.

The family as a social system changes according to its own history of evolving tasks. Each major transition in its life cycle offers a family the possibility to become something new.

—Every family transition is a crisis or turning point in which everything could get better or worse.
—Every family transition is marked by a sense of loss, confusion, anxiety, excitement, and adventure. Sometimes the transition generates chaos and disorganization in the family.
—Every family transition includes some sadness. Even when the change is desired or even inevitable, there will be loss. Grieving the loss is one way families adapt; promising again is another.
—Every family's capacity to grieve its anticipated, as well as unanticipated, losses will in large measure determine its ability to live through the crises of change.
—Every family responds to a transitional crisis according to their

Transitional Event	Leaving home events	Wedding	Birth of first child	Last child leaves	Death of a spouse
Family Tasks	Leaving home	Becoming married	Raising children	Promising again	Living alone
	Identity formation	Leaving home	Becoming married	Raising children	Identity re-formation
		Identity formation	Leaving home	Leaving home	Promising again
			Identity formation		

Figure 1. Transitions in the family life cycle

internal resources and the stress of the context. The key to coping with a transitional crisis is the ability to adapt.
—Every family transition intensifies the need for continuity in the midst of change. A family's capacity to respond to the discontinuities of change depends on living with paradox.

The family life cycle is the most practical and effective way of helping people understand the family as a social unit with a life and history of its own. It also provides a framework for thinking about how ordinary pastoral interventions related to the church's ritual life correspond to critical moments of transition in the family's history. The church's ministry with families often requires a delicate balance between attending to the needs of children and adults throughout their stages of development and the needs of the family as a whole that is itself experiencing change. If marriage preparation, for example, ignores the changes and contradictions in becoming married that evoke grief and sadness, it will impede rather than enhance the possibility that God is doing a new thing in forming this new family.

The emphasis in this series on family tasks and transitions is an alternative to the stage-specific approach to the changes, for example, in the history of a marriage. Books with titles such as *Surviving Family Life: The Seven Crises of Living Together* presume that "all families move through a cycle of stages, and each stage has built in predictable crises."[5] It is true that every marriage must endure significant change and some changes can be anticipated. It is equally true that the success or failure of a marriage depends on how they handle the crises those changes create. The emphasis on stages, however, does not allow enough flexibility to respond to the bewildering complexity that couples encounter in the course of marriage today. This discussion of the need for promising again through all the changes and crises of being married is intended to be a vision of hope for the future of our lives together.

Paradox in Family Living

We return again to the theme of paradox. Throughout this series, we have attempted to keep in paradoxical tension several seemingly contradictory statements that on further reflection are essentially true. Autonomy and community, being separate and being together, are paradoxically related in marriage and family living. That is the central paradox. Families that endure and thrive honor the autonomy of each member while at the same time promoting in a total way the well-being of the community as a whole. Understanding marriage as a pilgrimage of promising adds yet another nuance to the paradox of family living. We keep promises by changing them; we find life by letting it go. This is generally true for Christian living, but it is particularly necessary for sustaining a marriage over the life cycle.

Contradictions that are true are not accidental. They are inherent in human nature, in the circumstances of our lives, in the dynamics of family living. In a book titled *The Age of Paradox,* Charles Handy has observed that paradox is like the weather, something to be lived with, not solved. "Paradox has to be *accepted,* coped with and made sense of, in life, in work, in the community, and among nations."[6] Living with paradox need not confuse us even though it will often surprise us. Balancing the contradictions of family living, for example, is neither random nor haphazard. Promising again, as we shall develop it in this book, is a way of living with the paradox of marriage—to remain constant we must keep changing.

If change is central to the vitality of a family's life over time, paradox is what gives shape to its meaning and sustains its well-being in time. Paradox remains even when change occurs. It is inevitable and perpetual in family living. We have to leave home in order to make a home. Becoming married requires a balance between community and individual autonomy, between private and public realities, and between continuity and discontinuity with one's past. Families are likely to get in trouble when they do not keep alive both dimensions of the paradox. On the other hand, families remain vital if they can stay in the contradictions that finally only God can resolve.

Because people would rather stand on one side of a paradox or the other, our ministry with families may in fact require that we intensify the creative tensions by "saying the other side." It is our pastoral task to intend paradox precisely because the unresolvable contradictions in our lives often become the occasion for transformation. We believe that paradox is not just a therapeutic tool or a means to effect some new resolution, but an unavoidable reality in our lives as human beings. The helper's task is to assist people to live in the paradoxes of existence that are central to family well-being throughout the cycles of life.

In the end, promising is something we discover, as well as something we do. The paradox is this: promising is an experience of activity and passivity for we receive promises as well as make them. The promises we make to others are preceded by receiving God's promise that has already been made to us in our baptism. It is easier to receive promises when we believe that ordinary human promises embody the promise of God. The wedding, for example, is God's promised fidelity to a couple witnessed to by the community's presence. The activity of promising and promising again in marriage is therefore preceded by receiving that promise of God.

Acknowledgments

This series, Family Living in Pastoral Perspective, is the outcome of years of collaboration with Kenneth R. Mitchell. Unfortunately, Ken died suddenly of a heart attack on February 18, 1991, before this project could be completed. Although this volume has been written conjointly with David Hogue and Marie McCarthy, S.P., the spirit of Kenneth Mitchell is still very much present. We hope we have honored his memory by what we have written. I am grateful to the friends—both new and old—who have joined with me in completing this endeavor: *Becoming Married* with Robert Cotton Fite, *Regarding Children* with Susan B.W. Johnson, and *Living Alone* with Freda Gardner. The collaboration with each of these authors has enriched the project as a whole.

We are indebted to many people who have told us their stories about promising again. While the stories have been altered to preserve their anonymity and their real names do not appear, these people have been internal partners with us in writing this volume. The stories ascribed to Herbert, David, or Marie are, however, the actual stories of the authors.

I am particularly grateful to the thirty-eight students at Catholic Theological Union in my twentieth class on "The Pastoral Care of Families" for their willingness to walk with me in the completion of this manuscript. We are grateful to many friends and colleagues who have contributed ideas or stories and offered constructive criticism as this book evolved: Phyllis Anderson, David Breed, Evon Eckhoff, OFM, Mary Frohlich, Martha Jackson-Oppeneer, Richard Jensen, Susan B.W. Johnson, Douglas A. Larson, Patricia Mehler, Nancy Poling, Chris R. Schlauch, Carl D. Schneider, Karen Speerstra, and Diane Stephens—to name a few.

Adaptability of forms, clarity of communication, and flexibility of structures are necessary but not sufficient for the sake of marriage and family living today. Families are sustained not just by explicit rules, clear communication, or flexible structures, but by a vital spirit. Promising is soul work and like all effective soul work, it takes time. We enter that process, as we began the journey of writing this book, with the ringing promise from one of the lessons for Maundy Thursday. "Let us hold fast to the confession of our hope without wavering, for he who has promised is faithful" (Heb. 10:23). It is the faithfulness of God that guarantees our fragile promises and makes us bold enough to believe that promising again is a reason for hope for family living today.

HERBERT ANDERSON

Holy Week 1995

1

THE GIFT OF PROMISING

MAKING PROMISES is a common human activity. Each of us could write the story of our individual lives and the histories of our families according to promises made, kept, changed, broken, and made again. We promise to tell the truth, keep a secret, or be on time for dinner. We promise we will change our habits, that the hurt will go away, or that we will return the lawnmower tomorrow. Our promises are simple and profound, foolish and wise, formal and informal. We keep some promises; others we don't. Even when we fail, we promise again and then again. As the philosopher Hannah Arndt once observed, promising is the sacrament of the will. It is what humans do.

What we promise, how we promise, and how we keep promises change throughout life. When we were children, the promises we made were simple, concrete, and direct. They were also global and grand. Children can be more certain about their promises because they are usually not limited by the knowledge of what is possible. As we grow older, we modify our promises because we know more about the unpredictability of life and the undependability of people. What was once a simple, spontaneous *yes* is measured and sometimes muted by countless qualifications. Still, we keep making promises.

We know from experience that promises are easier to make than to keep. Because of forgetfulness, frailty, or human sin, as well as ongoing change, we do not or cannot keep all the promises we make. *Promising again generally occurs when there is a promise we cannot, have not, or ought not keep in the form in which it was made.* In that sense, promising again is a necessary aspect of all enduring relationships and communities not just because of human weakness but because people and circumstances change. Friendships, belonging to a voluntary organization, or remaining with the same company all regularly require recommitment. Whenever it occurs, the choice to promise again is the choice of hope over despair.

Dimensions of Promising in Marriage

The promises we make in marriage have many dimensions (See figure 2). The *primary* promise is foundational. The promise to love,

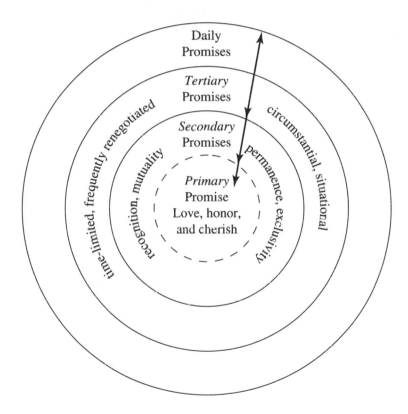

Figure 2. Three dimensions of promising in marriage. Note that the dotted line between primary and secondary promises is to suggest that these promises are closely linked together to form the fundamental or foundational promise.

honor, and cherish each other is a commitment to hold our covenant partner in abiding seriousness. This *primary* promise initiates the process of becoming married and defines the soul of the covenant. Although love deepens and takes different forms throughout the history of a marriage, it is the root metaphor for a marital bond that endures.

There are at least four *secondary* promises that grow out of and support the *primary* promise. Two of these have been traditionally linked with the covenant of marriage: (1) *Permanence*. The promise to love "until death parts us" creates an environment without conditions and (2) *Exclusivity*. Our pledge of faithfulness is a commitment to keep promising to one person and to the marriage itself. We have added two other *secondary* promises that reflect the fundamental commitment to honor the other person in marriage: (3) *Mutuality*. The aim is to foster a relationship in which reciprocal honor ends in mutual respect and equal regard and (4) *Recognition*. When we hold the marriage partner in abiding seriousness, we commit ourselves to a deep understanding of and respect for the uniqueness of the other.

The third dimension of promising is usually in response to particular circumstances or functions in family living. *Tertiary* promises are situational, time-limited, and negotiable. If a couple determines to keep one weekend each month free from any outside obligation, they are making a circumstantial promise that may be renegotiated. When a couple determines to stay together in marriage for the sake of child-rearing, that is a functional promise. If one parent agrees to stay home with young children so the other can invest fully in a career opportunity, that is a situational promise. When one partner sets aside his or her regular golf schedule while the other recovers from surgery, that is a time-limited response to a particular circumstance. It is at this level of promising where adaptation regularly occurs. One of the key elements to an enduring marriage is the capacity to make and modify circumstantial promises. However, marriages held together only by *tertiary* promises may survive but they are hollow in the center.

Most of the daily promises we make as a matter of course in family living flow from this *tertiary* dimension. When a parent promises to pick up a child after school for ballet lessons or for baseball practice, it is based on a prior functional agreement. If someone agrees to deposit money, order plane tickets, pick up the laundry, or arrange for a babysitter, they are making daily promises derivative of prior commitments that are both *primary* and *secondary*. If, however, daily promises are regularly broken or neglected, we are likely to ask questions about the *primary* promise. When a spouse forgets to pick up milk from the store or children from school, we may question his or her commitment to marriage itself rather than consider whether a secondary promise is still functional.

Two things are true. First, the promise to love and respect the other in a marital bond is foundational and unconditional. We give flesh to that promise through the changing, limited, daily promises of living together. The primary commitment to love and respect does not change, even though the forms of love and the depth of respect are re-formed as the people and the relationship change over time. In fact, the *primary* promise will continue only if it finds different expressions over time. We keep the promise by promising again. Second, when those expressive, derivative promises fail to live out the primary promise and our daily promises no longer nurture the foundation of the marital bond, even promising again is not enough. If the *primary* promise loses its connection to the other dimensions of promising, it may need to be transformed. We will return to this theme of transformation in the concluding chapter.

Remaining in the covenant of marriage is a process of promising again that occurs in response to the *secondary* dimension of marital commitment. We promise again in order to recognize and honor individual growth that has challenged our commitments and complicated the marital bond. We promise again when the gap between our vision and the reality of life together has become intolerable. We promise again because we learn more about life and ourselves than we knew when we made the *primary* promise. We promise again when a crisis occurs because the change creates an imbalance in the family that exceeds its coping resources. The gift of promising is the possibility of finding new ways of being married. Couples who practice the art of promising again are more likely to remain married until death parts them. This book bears the title *Promising Again* as a way of bringing into particular focus that major dynamic in the life of a marriage.

Promise Is a Verb and a Noun

There are a variety of words for the process we are calling "promising again." One such word is commitment. It is the more generic term. Rodney J. Hunter defines commitment as a binding social relationship "created by an act of promising, choosing, and self-giving" that is maintained by trust, hope, and a sense of moral obligation.[1] We make commitments to ideas as well as to people and to groups. Most definitions of commitment resemble promising because they imply persisting in a meaningful course of action or a relationship despite obstacles. Although there is considerable parallel between commitment and promising, we have chosen promising as the central theme for this book for at least three reasons. First, promising is more explicitly interpersonal than commitment or committing and hence amenable to a familial context because it insists on mutuality. Second, while both terms presume human agency, promising is more concrete than commitment and can therefore be more easily nuanced for the sake of family living. And third, it is more readily linked with the promises of God that precede all human promising. In the biblical tradition, promising is reinforced by themes of covenant, fidelity, and hopefulness.

When promise is a noun, it generally refers to a pledge or agreement or vow that implies future commitment to do or not to do something. A promise is something we send forward to guarantee future action. For example, when we say we will keep a promise, we bind ourselves for the future to a contract or agreement that has already been made. If a promise is regarded as an unchanging entity independent of the one making it, the focus is on the pledge rather than the one pledging. When theologian Louis Smedes writes about learning to live with the love we promise, his emphasis is on keeping commitments. "What finally comes of our commitments really depends on a thousand small choices we make in the *process* of keeping them."[2] Human communities are sustained, Smedes proposes, when people care enough to keep the commitments or promises that they dare to make.

When promise is a verb, it implies a relationship. "To promise" is the activity of making a pledge, giving one's word, or offering a guarantee. We promise to someone. When promising is understood more as verb than as noun, the focus shifts in three ways. First, the primary attention is on the person who does the promising rather than on the content, terms, and obligation of the promise. Second, the virtue or character that is expressed in the promising is as important as the promise itself. Third, it presumes that the promise, the promise makers, and the context keep changing. The image of *promising again* emphasizes the need to renew the promise and transform the promise keepers.

A promise is a pledge thrown ahead of us. For that reason, promising always has a future tense. It reflects a vision of human life and fulfillment that pulls us forward. A promise remains an obligation because we cannot take back what we promise. Promising is a religious activity that welcomes change and risks a future that God is continuing to make new. It is faith in the future of God that makes it possible to make promises in the present. But promising in the present is always a risk because we do not know the future. We have the courage to promise and promise again because we believe that the future toward which the whole creation is moving belongs to God.

Promising is an ongoing creative activity. The promises keep changing because the people change. We will fulfill the promise differently than we imagine because we keep changing as we live into the vision that is ahead. T. S. Eliot has captured this truth in these lines from "Little Gidding."

> And what you thought you came for
> Is only a shell, a husk of meaning
> From which the purpose breaks only when it is fulfilled
> If at all. Either you had no purpose
> Or the purpose is beyond the end you figured
> And is altered in fulfillment.[3]

This understanding of promising supports the possibility of *creative fidelity*. Creative fidelity is a way of promising with one another that promotes both the unity of marriage and the freedom for individual growth. The promise, then, is altered in its fulfillment. According to philosopher Gabriel Marcel, at the core of fidelity there must be something creative or novel that will counter the staleness that occurs whenever we focus our attention on constancy or continuity.[4] We cannot know the end of a marriage at its beginning. Our commitment to the marital covenant is held alongside our pledge to pursue a vision of personal integrity beyond any one form of promising faithfulness. This paradox is at the center of our understanding of promising.

The Characteristics of Promising

Ethicist Margaret A. Farley has identified ways of thinking about promising and commitment that also support the freedom to grow in faithful love, in her book, *Personal Commitments*.[5] From her writing, and from the work of others, we have identified five characteristics of the act of promising. It is (1) relational, (2) self-constituting, (3) limiting, (4) future-oriented, and (5) continual. Each characteristic describes a *habitus* or quality of being in community to be fostered rather than a skill to be mastered. For marriage, that means a willingness to keep promising as a way of living.

Relational

Promising is fundamentally a relational act. We promise to another. We place something of ourselves in the keeping of another when we make a promise. *The survival of the promises people make to one another depends on a sense of mutuality.* We bind ourselves to each other to strengthen human belonging and deepen human vulnerability. "Our yearning to belong to each other and to God," Farley has observed, "can be satisfied only through some form of mutual commitment."[6] In order for the promise to another to be experienced in a mutual way, the commitments we make must be expressed explicitly. Unspoken expectations, as we will note later, undermine mutuality in any kind of relationship. When we give our word as pledge, we give power to our words to call to us from the one to whom we have made a pledge. Community is formed and marital bonds are enhanced when promising is mutual and reciprocal.

Because the activity of promising is a relational act, it is also communal. A promise is a pledge that involves the self, the other, and the community that receives the pledge and sustains the relationship. When the promise is made privately, the community may not know of the relationship in ways that allow public support. The absence of sustaining communities in a society makes promising in marriage more and more difficult. From a religious perspective, we understand the community's presence as a sign of God's promise of fidelity to the couple. In that sense, the hard work of promising and promising again in marriage is preceded by receiving not only the commitment of the other and God, but the pledge of the community as well. The presence of community deepens the joy, distributes the sorrow, provides new perspectives on problems, diffuses conflicts, and provides support in times of crisis.

Self-Constituting

The paradoxical connection between autonomy and community, between separateness and togetherness, is reflected also in the act of promising. It is an act that is at once self-constituting and relational. Promising creates community and constitutes the self. It solidifies our belonging and shapes who we become. When we make a promise, we publicly declare who or what we intend to be and become, as well as to whom or to what we belong. If we do not commit ourselves to anyone, we do not become anyone.

We promise because we are human. That we promise also makes us human. What and how we promise determines the contours of our unique and particular humanity. *Promising is a human activity that forms identity as well as community.* Over time, we may become the person we have promised to be. This is most likely to happen if we engage the tension between stability and change, between the good of the self and the good of the community, between our vision of who we would be and how we have lived the promise in the midst of a changing context.

> When I met Jed, I was experienced beyond my years. I was like a race car, ready to run off in any direction, burn out, and then take off again. His stability gave me freedom; his love slowed me down; his honesty gave me time to think. I thought committing myself to one person would tie me down and domesticate me. Strangely, for me, the more promises I made to Jed, the more free I felt. I was free to choose him, make promises for myself, *and* have a vision for our life together. It was an unexpected gift of promising   (Melissa)

Constituting a self is not the same as self-actualization. In the act of promising, we establish ourselves as agents in living. Making a promise presumes intentionality. Melissa discovered that promising to another did not limit her freedom to be intentional. She learned that the self is formed as much by making choices as by fulfilling the choices made. We are not aware of all the forces that shape our choices. Even so, we regard our promises as intentional acts. Self-conscious willing is a critical dimension of the activity of promising by which personal identity comes into being. When we fail in our commitments or fall short of fulfilling the promises we make, something of our *self* is lost or dies. Perhaps that is the truth embedded in the childhood pledge, "cross my heart and hope to die!"

Each person who promises does so within the limits of his or her own developmental framework and social context. The child promises differently than the adult. An aging adult, whose options are limited, promises differently than a young adult whose future is an uncluttered horizon. A single parent who works two jobs to support her family must keep her options open. Because she does not feel free to say no, she may promise more readily than the parent with a spouse and financial security. A woman of color may be less expansive about promising than a white man of privilege because she has experienced a need for caution that he has not known. The privileged man does not expect to keep all the commitments he makes because no one in his world does. The activity of promising still is self-constituting, but the context changes the consequences and the necessity of promising.

Limiting

Promising implies an acceptance of limits. By our act of promising, we freely choose to limit ourselves. We cannot live out every possibility. We choose a context when we promise. We declare the particular path we will follow and freely choose the concrete realities and circumstances that the path or context entail. Decision, Sam Keen has observed, is a cutting-off. "I travel one path only by neglecting many. Actual existence is tragic, but fantastic existence (which evades choice and limitation) is pathetic."[7] We cannot live without limits. Because promising limits, it is often an experience of loss. We mourn what we will not be and places we will not see when we choose a particular path. It is not always easy to live within the limits that promising imposes. We may presume to avoid loss by refusing to make commitments. Unfortunately, in order to avoid the limits of making choices, we may avoid life altogether.

> Don't get me wrong. I love Ann and the kids. My life with them is very comfortable. Yet I am aware that I continue to keep my options open emotionally. It is possible that something better might come along. I have taken every opportunity to travel for the company. I love the glamour. I also fantasize about falling in love somewhere with someone I have not yet met. In the meantime, Ann and the kids keep on growing and changing. I am not sure that I know my family anymore, and I don't know myself either. I do know loneliness.   (Barton)

Barton has chosen a fantastic existence that avoids choice and limitation. In refusing to give himself to a real life with all of its limits, Barton ends up lonely and without any life at all. The pathos of his life is a consequence of his unwillingness to live with the limits that promising imposes. *When we promise, we limit ourselves because we give others a claim on our lives and our plans.* Our promising also sets limits, boundaries, and parameters to relationships and activities. Paradoxically, the limits of life enable us to become who we are.

Future-Oriented

Promising not only limits the present, but it binds us to a future that becomes less open even though it is still unknown. We promise because we recognize, however dimly, that our life circumstances will not always be as they are in the present. For that reason, every vow or promise has an implicit, unanswered question that accompanies it: Where will it take us and what will it ask of us? It is a risky thing to promise. Every wedding has this future perspective. We imagine particular futures for our life together and pledge ourselves to the hard work of bringing them about, but we do not know in the moment of promising what the promise will require of us.

The human act of promising is a discipline against future failure. It is a hoped-for remedy against inconsistency and uncertainty. We do not know the future. Nor can we be certain how we will act at some future time in relation to promises made in the past. As Margaret Farley observes, "Commitment as it appears in the human community implies a state of affairs in which there is doubt about our future actions."[8] Promising is an acknowledgment of our inability to know how we will respond to what the future may demand of us. We will not be as reliable and as faithful as we wish. We promise because we know that our will is not always firm and that we are not always consistent.

Sometimes we make promises in order to guarantee a particular future against the possibility of unknown chaos. Our insistence on keeping a promise in such circumstances becomes a way of predicting the future in order to control indeterminacy. Children, for example, identify the promise with its outcome. The child whose outing did not turn out as planned will cajole parents with the tearful phrase "but you promised . . . " We do need to anticipate future circumstances in order to cope with inevitable change, but promising for the sake of controlling the future is an act of unfaith. We cannot equate the promise with its outcome. Such a promise must be broken for the sake of God's future. When the future is the focus, the most we can promise is that we will keep promising despite the uncertainty. And be willing to be surprised.

Continual

This continuing character of promising has at least two meanings. Our promising is never a finished product. We make a promise in a relatively brief, contained space of time, but we spend a lifetime actualizing the meaning of the promise. In that sense, the act of promising is ongoing. It occurs in all the daily promises people make to one another that derive from commitments made at the *tertiary* level of promising. There is probably no other human community in which this ongoing activity is more present and necessary than in the continual promising of two people to each other in marriage.

> It used to be that when someone asked me if I was married, I would simply answer, "Yes." But I've learned that the answer is different at different times in my life. Now when someone asks me if I'm married, I answer, "A little bit," or "hardly at all," or "more than ever." (Desmond)

Desmond's answer is profoundly accurate. It captures the shifting that ordinarily occurs in the marital bond as people change. This is the second meaning of continual. He has found a way to express the permanent instability of being married. He, however, may be covering anxiety with cleverness. We can only assume that Desmond understands promising as continual because the context, the promisor, and the one to whom he promised keep changing. As Gabriel Marcel has observed, "I cannot be sure my inner disposition will not change." [9] It is difficult to promise a future we do not see. We can only wager on it and then make the promise over and over again, because the future seldom works out just as we imagined.

Each of these five characteristics of promising are grounded in trust and hope. Although promising is a way of giving structure to an unknown future, we need to be prepared to be surprised. The ends we imagined are always altered in fulfillment, not only because people change but because God continues to make all things new. It takes courage and trust to keep promising when constancy is not likely and the future cannot be prescribed. Promising is a hopeful act because it presumes that tomorrow does not have to be the same as yesterday. Growth and change need not doom a marriage. The possibility of promising again is thus a sign of hope because we are not trapped by the past.

Why Promise Again

What we promise one another in marriage is that we will continue to promise. That is part of the nature of promising. Promising again is a necessity because of the inevitability of change. We either promise again to another in friendship and marriage or a relationship stagnates and dies. Promising again is a necessary dimension of all enduring relationships because people and circumstances change. It is common in our culture to buy new machines or appliances when they break down. We are tempted to do the same when marriages flounder. This book is based on the belief that we must renegotiate our covenants in order to keep them.

Promising again involves other benefits besides durable bonds. It is a way of deepening our intimacy with those we live with and love. We become clearer about our own personal identity when we are challenged to redefine ourselves in our relationships. Because promising again is also oriented toward the other person, we may become less self-oriented as we learn the art of self-transcendence. Promising again, as we will explore in the concluding chapter, is a prelude to transformation. It keeps us tending toward those relationships of vulnerability in which self-transformation is most likely to occur.

Every successful relationship requires the ability to adjust to change. In an essay about couples facing retirement, family therapists Salvador Minuchin and Michael P. Nichols make an observation that is true throughout marriage. "Whatever type of balance a couple [or a family] work out, their relationship will need to be rebalanced at traditional points in the life cycle."[10] Every couple must have a formula for stability and a formula for change. Some of the changes that require rebalancing are expected, anticipated, and somewhat predictable. These changes may be so incremental that they are hardly noticed. Or the growth that occurs because of the change is so welcome in the family that it cancels out any inconvenience or discomfort the change may produce. Most families have the resources to cope with ordinary moments of transition in the life cycle.

Sometimes, however, the changes, whether expected or unexpected, are so stressful that the family is thrown into a crisis requiring serious adaptation just to keep a steady state. The change requires more adaptation than the system can provide. Just continuing the initial promise of marriage is not enough. The following sampling of changes in marriage illustrate their pervasiveness. All these changes, those we expect and those we do not expect, those we choose and those we do not choose, those we can manage and those we cannot, press us to examine the need for promising again.

—The family decides to make room for an aging grandparent who can no longer live alone.
—Mother and father decide to welcome back into their home a young adult son struggling with addiction or a daughter who has decided to leave her husband.
—Mother chooses the opportunity to accept a new job that requires the family to move to a new city, or father decides to become a freelance photographer.
—The family home is destroyed by fire.
—A teenage daughter is raped on a date.
—The company downsizes, and suddenly the family loses its stable income.
—A son comes home to die because he has AIDS.
—A child dies suddenly because of illness or an accident.

We know these things happen, but we do not expect that they will happen to us. *Because the discontinuity engendered by these changes is enough to destabilize the system, these kinds of crises in the family require couples to promise again in order to keep the balance.*

The same practice of promising again is necessary in any community sustained by voluntary commitments. The following story from outside marriage illustrates the need to promise again when *secondary* and *tertiary* promises change.

> When I entered the Sisters of Providence at age seventeen, I was young and inexperienced. It was 1960. The Second Vatican Council had not yet opened, and the winds of change had not yet hit the Church or the religious community that I joined. By the time I pronounced my final vows in 1968, everything was up for grabs. All the external structures of religious life were being shaken. Rules were changing. Habits were changing. Customs were changing. Centuries-old traditions were changing. It was a time when the possibility of permanent commitment was being questioned everywhere. After considerable soul searching and conversation about my own doubts and the uncertainty of the future, I came to the realization that I could only promise to follow as faithfully as I could wherever it was that God was leading me.   (Marie)

As Marie's religious community continued to change and as she continued to grow, being faithful to her life in that community meant promising again and again. That is something different than keeping a promise. It is the way of *creative fidelity*. Marie has had to promise again to her religious community in order to respond fully and faithfully to God's action in her life. Despite all the changes, the primary promise of fidelity to God's call remained constant. Husbands and wives must likewise keep promising in order to be faithful to one another and to God. None of us knows in the beginning where our promising will take us. What we do know is that we must continue promising again and again as the circumstances of our lives continue to change.

What Is Promising Again?

Promising again, as we use it in this volume, is *a revitalization of promising, finding the way in the midst of our human limits and changing circumstances to transform both the promise and the promise maker*. When the discontinuities of our marital lives are so significant or the family crisis so full of anguish, we must renegotiate the covenant in order to keep it.

Beyond the Initial Promise

Promising again is not the same as making a new promise or making many promises in the hope that one will work. Neither is promising again simply starting over. Rather, it is an act of fidelity beyond the initial promise. Promising again is an act of *creative fidelity* because we see and understand implications and dimensions of the initial promise we could never have anticipated when we first made it. It is a courageous act born of vigor, sturdiness of character, and the determination to see something through in the best possible way we can. When we promise again, we look beyond the terms of the promise to each partner as a promising person and to the relationship that is being promised.

Promising again moves beyond constancy to fidelity. Constancy in human covenants is often sustained by perseverance, and may reflect a refusal to be open to new possibilities. Fidelity, on the other hand, is an exercise of imagination that seeks out new avenues, alternate approaches, and creative pathways of fidelity. Sometimes, as Margaret Farley has observed, we need "to find another way to love justly, perhaps another framework in which to incarnate the expression and the strivings of the original love" when the original ways no longer work.[11] *Just as our initial promises create community and shape character, our promising again represents a fidelity to the self we have promised to be within the communities we are committed to sustain.*

There are occasions in the life of every family when we cannot see a promise through in the way we once thought we could or would. The circumstances have changed so radically that we must see the meaning and the requirements of our promising in a whole new way. It is not easy to decide when the sacrifice required to keep the promise is so great that it frees one from obligation to the promise.

> We had promised that we would take care of each other always so that neither of us would ever have to go into a nursing home. When Edgar began to deteriorate, some part of me was dying too. Eventually he didn't know me anymore. He became belligerent and increasingly difficult to handle. I could not manage his care, but I would not break our promise. Caring for him at home was taking an enormous toll on me and on the kids, who were trying to help out as much as they could. When I finally realized that the circumstances of his life had taken us beyond the promise, I could let him be taken to a nursing home. Still, I cried more on the day they took him to a special nursing home than I did when he died eight months later.
>
> (Frances)

It took Frances a long time to understand that if she was to be faithful to the one to whom she had promised, as well as to the person she had promised to be, she would have to live out her promise to Edgar in a way she had never planned. She wanted and intended to be faithful to Edgar. Sometimes, as illustrated by the story of Frances, in order to renew our commitment to a concrete, realistic love, we must go beyond the initial promise. For Frances, changing the terms of the promise was the only way to fulfill it. *Every change we face as a family, expected or unexpected, planned or unplanned, demands an act of promising again when the discontinuity is greater than the continuity.*

It is not always easy to know when changing the framework of a commitment represents an act of fidelity and when it represents irresponsibility or betrayal. There are times when fidelity demands that we change. Some of those changes are internal. We change inwardly, see things in new ways, and reinvest more fully in our own actions. The external circumstances may appear much the same to the casual observer because the changes are within. At other times, the external factors may change while we continue to be more fully the person we have promised to be. The continuity is within when we keep a promise to the other and to ourselves by changing its terms according to a changed context. That is what we understand as *creative fidelity*.

Breaking Promises

Some promises ought to be broken, because keeping them may represent the ultimate infidelity. Some of our promises are made in haste. Others are made wrongly. Some are made with too little knowledge of ourselves, the one to whom we promise, or the situation in which we promise. Still others are made because of arrogance or pride. We know with great sorrow that there are times when we must break a promise we have made. The principle that Margaret Farley invokes in making these very complicated decisions is that "while we may sacrifice everything we have, we may not sacrifice everything we are."[12] We break some promises in order to promise again. We never do it lightly, but do it we must in some instances in order to keep faith with God and with ourselves.

> As long as I can remember, I have loved to learn. As a child, I waited for the lending-library van as eagerly as I waited for the ice-cream man. I had just finished junior college when I married Delbert. We had four children in a hurry, so I did not have time or energy to read. I was also too busy to be bothered by Delbert's constant verbal abuse. Nothing I did was ever good enough. When our youngest started school, my parents gave me money to take a college course. Delbert hit me for the first time when he found out I was going back to school. That incident began a spiral of physical abuse that lasted until I moved out three years later. (Madeline)

Much could be said about the complexities of marriage today, based on the story of Madeline and Delbert. The loss of power or control that often precedes physical violence in the family is only one illustration of fundamental gender changes in family living today. Our focus, however, is on promising. The story of Madeline is one occasion when the obligation of self-respect and self-care supersedes the commitment to a marriage that has become destructive. All the hope Madeline could muster, all the faith in the future she could call on, all the straining to see, and all the remembering and forgetting that she had practiced for years did not prove to be enough for her to keep the promise. Keeping a promise in its old form would have been an act of infidelity to herself, to Delbert, and to her children.

There are some circumstances in which breaking the promise is an act of *creative fidelity*. For instance, if a spouse walks out after twenty years of marriage, files for divorce, and remarries, it is not possible for the marital partner to sustain the initial promise. Divorce itself can be a fidelity, a way of keeping a promise by finding a newer, deeper, often more difficult and painful way to keep faith with oneself. Likewise, a second marriage after a divorce can be an act of faith and hope as we promise again, in the midst of our own limitations and failures, to see our promises through as we had hoped and pledged.

Leaving one's religious order in the Roman Catholic tradition can also be an act of fidelity. If the commitment one has made to religious life as a way of serving God leads to a smallness of soul and vision rather than to service among God's people, fidelity to the commitment to serve God supersedes the promise to remain in religious life.

> I did a life review with my spiritual director in preparation for the celebration of fifty years as a member of a Roman Catholic religious community. What I discovered shocked me. I had never really lived my own life. I had spent a lifetime doing and being for others but I had never addressed the questions of life for myself. I was sixty-eight years old, a highly skilled and educated professional. I had been respected as a school principal for twenty years. Even so, I did not know how I would support myself in the outside world. Nonetheless, I decided to leave my religious community before my golden jubilee in order to discover what I might become. Even though I left the community, I still understood I was being faithful to God even though I had broken my promise. (Clara)

Clara's decision to leave her community is a poignant illustration of the paradox of promising. She broke a pledge that she had kept for almost fifty years in order to promise again a fidelity to the deepest meaning of the covenant in which she had lived all those years. If we do not live the contradictions embedded in the promises we make, we may never know where they will lead us. The journey that our promises begin and that is sustained by promising again is seldom easy, and the end of the journey is almost always a surprise.

Throughout moments of crisis and change in our lives, we continue to ask ourselves, Who will I become if I keep this promise? And who will I become if I change this promise or if I break this promise? Ordinary changes in ordinary living continue to push us to make a new promise. We are always in a new context, a new situation, a new time. We are different. And our promising must be different as well. For that reason, we believe that very few promises can or ought to be kept in their original form or within the concrete terms of the initial promises. And sometimes it is necessary to break a promise in order to promise again, pledging one's self and one's fidelity to a new relationship, wagering again on the possibility that we can be faithful to this love.

When Do We Promise Again?

The first answer to the question When do we promise again? should be evident by now. Couples or communities must promise again whenever there is a crisis precipitated by change dramatic enough to threaten their coping skills. Sometimes, by the time people get to promising again, the emotional resources of the family have been used up or positive sentiments worn thin by coping with the conflict or crisis. Couples may wait too long to begin the hard work of renegotiating and renewing the marital bond. In order to overcome this difficulty, we suggest that people in marriage, or other relationships, need to anticipate the ordinary changes that may precipitate a crisis so they can begin the process of promising again before emotions are frayed or resources depleted.

The fundamental assumption behind our emphasis on promising again is the inevitability of paradox in every aspect of human living. We understand that marital bonds need to keep changing in order to remain constant. Charles Handy, in his book *The Age of Paradox,* has suggested that one pathway through paradox is to build a new future while we maintain the present. It is a way of promising again. The sigmoid curve, according to Handy, is an S-shaped curve that sums up the story of life itself (see figure 3). It is as true for the course of love and relationships as it is for empires and corporations. "We start slowly, experimentally, and falteringly; we wax and then we wane."[13]

The secret to constant growth, according to Handy, is to start a new sigmoid curve before the first one "peters out." The place to start the second curve is at point *A* while there is time and energy and resources "to get the new curve through its initial explorations and flounderings before the first curve begins to dip downward."[14] Even though they are connected, the second curve will be noticeably different from the first.

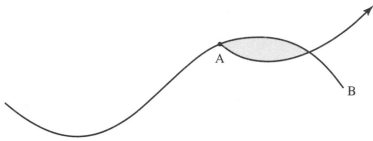

Figure 3. Sigmoid curve in promising again

The second curve, we suggest, is an illustration of promising again. Here is how Handy himself makes the connection to marriage.

> A good life is probably a succession of second curves, started before the first curve fades. Lives and priorities change as one grows up and older. Every relationship will sometimes need its second curve. Too often, couples cling to their old habits and contracts for too long. By the time they realize the need for that second curve they are already at point *B*. It is too late to do it together. They find other partners. On the other hand, I sometimes like to say, teasingly, that I am on my second marriage—but with the same partner.[15]

Being married again in this way to the same partner is one example of promising again. Launching children is another. As children are leaving home, we need to begin a new way of being family before the old one disappears and wives and husbands wonder why they are still married. Any major change in a family's history could become the occasion to begin a second curve, even before the change becomes a crisis. Promising again is a kind of "second-curve thinking" that provides a regular pathway through the paradox of marriage and family living today. In an age of turbulence and rapid change, the secret to promising again for the sake of constancy in marriage is to allow the past and the future to coexist in the present.

The Paradox of Promising Again

Paradox is the constant condition of human life in the light of God. According to the philosopher Jacob Needleman, God has placed the deepest and most fundamental contradictions in human life "not to be resolved but to be lived in the full consciousness of their contradictoriness."[16] The human story of promising is necessarily paradoxical. The act of promising again, when it is an expression of *creative fidelity,* is one of those contradictions meant to be lived rather than solved. We discover again and again that we need to change the content and terms of the promise in order to be faithful to the covenant that the promise implies at a deeper level.

There are four things Handy says about using the "sigmoid curve" as a pathway through paradox that are relevant for promising again in this deeper way.

1. *You will know where you are on the curve when you look back.* We will return to this theme in another chapter when we suggest that remembering the initial promise is a necessary part of promising again. Among other things, looking back helps us locate the present within a historical process. For our purposes, we also need to emphasize that taking seriously a change or loss is a way of marking where you are on the curve. The moment a significant change occurs in the life of a marriage may be the beginning of a second curve.

2. *Keeping the two curves going will become a habit.* Paradox will not go away. It is clear that schools and corporations need to develop a future direction while they are being successful in the present. The same, we suggest, is true of marriage. In that sense, we cannot wait for a crisis to precipitate the need to reconsider and renew the marriage. The old adage "if it ain't broke, don't fix it" no longer works. Couples will develop the habit of keeping two curves going as they allow the past and the future to coexist in their present.

3. *If one is too emotionally attached to what has gone before, it is difficult to change in any way.* One of the marks of promising again is letting go. The inability to let go of old images of a spouse, old hurts, old anger keeps couples stuck in the original curve. Couples may begin a second curve in marriage by determining to let go of unkept promises or unspoken expectations that continue to impede the present.

4. *By the time you know where you ought to go, it's too late to go there.* That is the ultimate paradox of promising again. Couples who insist on going on the same way they have been going will miss new opportunities for the future. The ways that got us to where we are seldom are those that will keep us where we want to be or allow us to go where we want to go. A word of caution from Handy about "second-curve thinking" is in order. We must be careful not to abandon the first curve too early. That is to say, the future of a marriage needs to be rooted in

its past if it is to be real.[17] Couples need resources and time to initiate a new future together. In a way, "second-curve thinking" makes promising again the norm for family living in modern times.

The paradox of promising again lies in the reality that the fulfillment of our promising often takes a different form than we imagined when we first pledged ourselves. It is this paradoxical understanding of promising that leads to the possibility of *creative fidelity.* Our experience of promising and promising again often takes us beyond the end we imagined, as T. S. Eliot has observed. Divorce, as well as the remarriage, may be understood as an act of promising again, in which people pledge themselves in the deepest possible way to an integrity beyond particular, concrete circumstances and beyond any one form of living out the promise. When we allow our promising again to be shaped by the possibility and inevitability of change, the end will almost always be "altered in fulfillment."

God's Faithfulness Is also Paradoxical

In this chapter we have explored the various issues related to promising and promising again as a general human process. In subsequent chapters, we will reexamine the dynamics of promising in relation to significant moments in a family's history. We believe it is crucial in order to stay married in our time that couples learn to practice the art of promising again and again. We have used the term *promising again* rather than *keeping promises* because we need not continue every promised relationship at any cost in order to be faithful people. Nor are promises always kept in the same way they were made. Our commitment to the covenant of marriage and to the individual with whom we live the lifelong marital promise is held alongside our pledge to pursue a vision of personal integrity beyond any one understanding of fidelity. Inner fidelity and systemic stability are always paradoxically linked. That is *creative fidelity.*

Promising again is an ethical act because it is about making choices in the midst of a crisis. The choices we make are shaped more by personal virtue and a common vision than by obligation and duty. In these reflections about promising, we have also sought to find a way of living out relationships with others in which God's loyalty is the ultimate model and criterion. Although God's steadfastness is beyond human possibility, nonetheless it is the aim of Christians living in any human covenant to embody God's loyalty. We honor God by our willingness to be faithful. We honor God's faithfulness when we choose to promise again.

There is a wonderful paradox in divine loyalty that is a gracious word for human promising. Biblical theologian Katharine Doob Sakenfeld has suggested that divine loyalty can never be taken for granted even though it is abounding. Despite the long history of God's forbearance with human disobedience, "each occasion of disobedience raised anew the possibility that the people might be cast off forever. The royal theology settled this problem by emphasizing the permanence of God's covenant."[18] God's loyalty is always promised yet always a surprise.

Human promising is no less paradoxical. Fidelity is a gift and a surprise even when it occurs in a committed covenant of marriage. When marital love is taken for granted because the promise is "until death parts us," the daily expressions of the *primary* promise are forgotten or neglected. Because human promising is fragile, we cannot assume that any marital promise is forever. If, however, we believe that the marital bond is a conditional contract, ordinary promises are clouded by daily anxiety. We need the security of permanence in order to love freely. Like God's loyalty, marital love is always promised yet always a surprise.

The faithfulness of God is more than a model. God is the guarantor of the promise. Sakenfeld puts it this way. "In experiencing God's faithfulness, we find strength to keep trying to live loyally in the midst of human confusion and uncertainty, in the midst of opposition, in the midst of dejection and frustration."[19] Our best fidelity is more fragile than we like to admit. Nonetheless, our weakness and uncertainty should not paralyze us. We make our promises to one another trusting in God's enduring loyalty.

2
WHEN THE NEST
IS EMPTYING

THERE ARE particular moments in the life cycle of a family when promising again is necessary for the sake of a marriage. The addition of children to a family is one such time. The changes that occur when parenting begins are significant enough that husbands and wives need to be intentional about recommitting to one another in light of those changes. The next life cycle moment for promising again occurs when children are being launched and parenting changes. This transitional moment begins when the first child leaves and continues until the last child is settled outside the home. The ease with which couples adapt to this transition depends on how empty the nest feels.

> When our son Andrew left for college, I was prepared to buy less milk and ice cream, cook less food, wash less laundry, and worry less. My Friday nights were free in the fall because I did not have to go to football games. I had more time to myself in the winter because I did not have swimming meets to attend or play rehearsals to monitor. The telephone rang less often, a tank of gas lasted longer, and there were fewer arguments at dinner. I was, however, unexpectedly disturbed by the quiet. Sometimes it seemed like living in a morgue. My husband and I did have more choices on movies to rent. Home life was generally less complicated. It took us awhile to realize we did not need to retreat to the bedroom for privacy. We enjoyed our new freedom, but I never thought a lighter load would feel so heavy. (Marjorie)

Letting children go is both sad and liberating. The feelings evoked by the experience are a mixture of relief and grief. The house is quieter, but parents will say, as Marjorie did, that the quiet is deafening. Dinner is more peaceful, but sometimes it is sustained by long, awkward pauses in the conversation. The loss felt when children leave evokes a sense of emptiness. Even parents who have looked forward to these changes as opportunities for marital intimacy are likely to agree with Marjorie: The lighter load is heavier than they thought it would be.

The length of this launching or leaving-home moment is elastic. It may be prolonged if adult children do not leave or postponed because they return home for financial or emotional support. Each family will have its own criteria for determining when children are truly settled outside the home: being gainfully employed, marrying, owning a home, or having a child. The leaving-home moment is prolonged in a second marriage where husbands and wives and their respective children are of different ages. Shifting gender roles, an unstable job market, expectations of affluence, and persisting individualism intensify the need for promising again at any time, but they also complicate the process by which husbands and wives reaffirm or renegotiate their understanding of being married.

When two people promise to love one another in marriage until death parts them, they intend to be faithful over time, through changing circumstances, in difficult places. Promising again enables a couple to sustain their promises to one another over time, despite the inevitable changes that are part of family living. Each individual changes and, as a result, the relationship changes. The environment of a marriage does not remain constant over time. Often, however, the most dramatic family changes occur during the moment when the nest is emptying. "The family must confront its shrinking size, recoup from the shock of profound losses, and acknowledge that the family is undergoing the most radical transformation of its history."[1] The durability of a marital bond depends on promising again in light of all those changes.

Emptying the Nest

The life-cycle moment when adult children leave home has frequently been characterized with the metaphor of "the empty nest." The idea that a home (that is, the nest) is empty when children leave (even though two people continue to live in it) implies that raising children is the primary purpose of the family. According to this view, when children are launched, the family's work is done. The family is empty of its purpose, and there is little need for promising again.

This image of the empty nest has survived several decades and many revisions of textbooks on marriage. One family sociologist, Evelyn Duvall, continues to identify two stages that are initiated by this transition. Launching or leaving home is the first stage. It begins when the first child leaves home as a young adult and "ends with the empty nest" as the last child leaves home to live independently.[2] The second stage, which Duvall describes as "middle-aged parents in an empty nest,"[3] begins with the departure of the last child from the home and continues until the retirement or death of one of the spouses.

The persistence of the so-called empty nest has negative overtones for family living today. It exaggerates an ordinary crisis by emphasizing what is missing. It continues to foster a belief in the centrality of childrearing that no longer fits with the modern family. Because we understand the family as an environment in which adults as well as children are held and supported in order to grow and flourish, we do not regard a home without children as an empty nest. The size of the family unit may shrink, along with the milk bill and parental headaches, when adult children are launched, but one or two people still live at home. Moreover, the nest is emptying but never empty because it is always full of people and their stories.

Although Duvall observes correctly that half of the life of a marriage may be lived out without children as middle-aged and older adults, she continues to describe the nest as empty. If couples have remained married in order to fulfill a *tertiary* or functional promise for the sake of the children, the emptying nest moment intensifies the need to review the bond. In response to experiences that threaten the fundamental promise, couples may negotiate another functional or situational promise (such as recreational compatibility or economic stability) or they may address the deeper needs of their relationship by transforming the *primary* promise. We will return to this theme of transformation in chapter 6.

Childrearing, Leaving Home, and Promising Again

The emptying nest transition is the conclusion of a process that begins when children are first welcomed into the home. Two things are simultaneously true. *Parents have new freedom to attend to their relationship when sons and daughters leave home, and children leave home more easily when they see their parents discovering or looking forward to the renewal of their marital bond.* Leaving home and promising again are therefore inextricably linked together. The emotional separation between children and parents around leaving home is a transitional crisis that affects, and is affected by, the vitality of the marital bond.

> Near the end of the novel *For Love,* by Sue Miller, Lottie has returned to her second husband Jack after a tumultuous time away. Her marriage to Jack has not been as vital as the affair they had while Jack's wife was dying of cancer. Megan, Jack's youngest daughter, who still lives at home, has been antagonistic toward Lottie from the beginning of the marriage. When Megan announces that she is going on the road with an older man who plays in a rock band, Jack and his daughter disagree. Jack and Lottie, however, are in agreement. They are eager for Megan to leave. Lottie feels some relief that Jack has joined her in this matter. It seems to be a turning point in their life together. But, the author muses, "Who can say for certain whether Megan began to pull away so hard because she sensed their turn to each other? or whether they began to turn to their life together because Megan began to pull away?"[4]

The answer to both of Lottie's questions is yes. This story points to the reciprocity between the task of leaving home and that of promising again. In a sense, parents and children alike are individuating because both are leaving behind previous ways of living and relating. For parents, it means they reaffirm or rediscover their relationship as husband and wife. For adult children, it is a time of adventure that means leaving behind familiar roles and taking their places in the world. However, the focus of this book is on the changes parents must make to continue to live together in creative ways as a marital pair when children leave.

When a marital pair has neglected the relationship because they have been preoccupied with the tasks of parenting, the role shifts that take place when children leave home will challenge the adaptive capacities of the marriage. If the marital bond is strained or conflicted when this transition occurs, one of three things can happen: First, the child whose role it is to keep the marriage together may choose not to leave home. Second, couples may divorce when they discover that their relationship is intolerable without the mediating presence of children. Third, if the marriage has not solidified and promising again does not seem possible, the family may also mobilize itself to hold on to the last child. *The dread of abandonment that makes it difficult for parents to let their children leave is a sign that the personal identity of one or both spouses is vulnerable and the marital relationship is impoverished.*

Promising again is complicated when adult sons and daughters come back after they have left or when they do not leave at all. For many adult children, continuing to live at home is either a matter of convenience or an economic necessity. Other adult children are emotionally linked to their first families in such a way that it is difficult for them to leave. Because entering the world of work today is objectively difficult, it is not always obvious which crises that keep adult children home are legitimate and which are an unhealthy emotional dependence on parents.

> I thought my son would become a plumber too and I could retire and leave him the business. It's a good business. But he wants to be an actor. He tells his mother in great detail about his auditions, and then he leaves with her all depressed and wanting him home again. Then, just when the two of us are settling back to normal and I'm grilling a steak and she is telling about her day in great detail, my son comes home again. He was a flop and the play was a flop, but the story is good for three more days of conversation between them. When he is not home, Connie and I agree that he ought to take a job and keep it for a while. But it is always the same. The moment he walks through the door, she is his Mom again.   (Kyle)

Connie and Kyle are not alone. It is difficult for fathers and mothers to know when they need to keep parenting and when their continuing to parent is hindering their children from leaving home. Sometimes parents who presume to give their children independence actually foster the opposite. Children become more dependent, even though that is not what parents say they want. For adult children who have been convinced by their parents or their own experience that the world is a frightening or complex place, home is a place of safety, and parents are an emotional lifeline. Kyle's story is repeated even when parents insist that they cannot wait for their children to leave. And adult children who do not want the family to change, often find ways to sabotage the efforts of their parents to promise again.

It Won't Be the Same after You're Gone

The departure of children changes things. The most obvious change occurs in family roles. *Active parenting is diminished.* The second change is less obvious. There are *fewer alliances available in the household on a daily basis.* Third, *there is greater freedom* for both husbands and wives as their children leave home. Each of these changes reverses what was identified in an earlier book in this series, *Regarding Children,* as necessary adaptation when children are added.[5] The departure of children creates a crisis of subtraction rather than addition. And for many parents, this process of letting go is more difficult to live through than adding roles or tasks to the family.

When Active Parenting Is Less

The transition to parenthood is one of the most critical tasks husbands and wives face when children are added to a family. The movement from daughter or son to wife or husband, and then on to mother or father requires a capacity to add new roles to one's self-understanding. The ease with which those new roles are internalized in part depends on the ability to separate from our homes of origin. *When it is done well, leaving home makes it easier to marry and become parents. In a similar way, effective marital bonding makes it easier to launch adult children and relinquish the parenting role.*

> Our children were slow to leave home. All of them lived with us for some time after they finished college. We considered it a sign of their trust and affection that they were comfortable at home when so many of their friends constantly battled with their parents. They are all living on their own now, but Verona and I still talk about them far into the night. Our youngest child is having the most difficult time getting by in life. Our middle daughter lives some distance from home, but both of us talk to her several times a week in order to provide practical and emotional support. Because my son and I are in the same line of work, we connect regularly around work issues. I am glad that Verona does not have to work outside the home so she can be ready to help our children whenever they ask. It gives us a great deal of pleasure to be able to provide financial support for our children in ways that our parents could not support us. After three years, we still miss having the kids around.
>
> (Derwin)

The relationship between Derwin and Verona and their three children is unclear. It is a positive thing when parents actively miss having their grown children around. Moreover, it is beneficial to be able to provide financial and emotional support for children who are getting launched. The extent of their contact with their children and the amount of time they spend talking about them both suggest that Derwin and Verona have not as yet given up being actively involved in the parenting role. They would appear still to be involved enough in parenting that the need to promise again is not apparent.

When children leave home, husbands and wives are forced to look at each other without the shadows of children to blur the distance between them. It is as if a cloak has been removed and old flaws are visible, old wounds hurt again, and unmet dreams for marriage from long ago are revived. It is also a potential identity crisis if the self-understanding of a spouse depends on preserving the parenting role. Couples frequently will avoid confronting this inevitable crisis by re-focusing attention on their adult children. If the identity of each spouse and the stability of the marital bond depend on keeping the parenting role alive, husbands and wives will find ways to stay actively involved in the lives of their adult children in order to keep parenting. When that happens, promising again, as we understand it, may be postponed.

Shifting Alliances Again

The addition of children changes the existing marital bond and alliances that may have formed among siblings or between children and one or both parents. The task of welcoming children into a family includes establishing a process of shifting alliances so no one becomes the permanent outsider. *In effective families, alliances shift and togetherness always moves around.* When they do not shift, family members are likely to seek new alliances outside the home. For husbands or wives, that often results in having an affair.

> It began shortly after my mother died. I was an only child and the center of my mother's life. Although she made demands on my life that I regularly resented, my mother was nonetheless my steady ally. My wife, Delia, was preoccupied with being mother to our children. She was not as supportive to me as my own mother. My relationship with Joanne began because we both enjoyed reading aloud to one another. I had not planned for it to become a sexual relationship. When it was over, I knew I had been looking for something. (Martin)

Martin's story adds yet another dimension to the alliances that keep shifting in families. If the leaving-home process is incomplete for one or both of the spouses, their parents will continue to play an active role in the alliances that are formed in a family. Martin's wife was a permanent outsider in the family because of Martin's primary alliance with his mother. In this situation, Martin's children were not a factor. In other situations, the addition of a child or children may identify one parent as the permanent outsider unless family alliances keep shifting.

The departure of children means that alliances must change again. Couples are not always prepared for the new demands on the marital bond after children leave. Women who have waited for the freedom to do things for themselves after the children are gone become frustrated by men whose careers have peaked and who now want to invest more energy in the marriage. Men are disappointed that the intimacy they were hoping for after the children leave does not materialize. When women enter the career track late or men are forced to make a mid-life career change, husbands and wives who desire to promise again face complex choices.

When sons and daughters have had a hand in preserving their parents' marriage, it is difficult to let them go. In those instances, launching children will destabilize a marriage. Couples are not compelled to face each other as long as they can continue to communicate through their children. Sometimes this pattern of triangulating children to balance the marital bond is not apparent to the couple until it is too late to rectify it. *The departure of children creates a crisis for every set of parents that requires a reconsideration of the marital alliance.* Couples are most likely to flounder if they do not examine hidden or unarticulated expectations of what will change when children are launched.

New Freedom

The addition of children limits the family's freedom. Although some families expect only one parent to make most of the sacrifices that childrearing requires, the limits to freedom that accompany the arrival of a child need to be shared by everyone in the family that seeks for justice. One of the factors that makes a marriage just is mutual compromising, in terms both of who compromises and who benefits from it. However, the complexity of modern life in the workplace as well as in the home makes it difficult to share equally in childrearing.

The departure of children creates new freedom for parents. When parental responsibilities have been shared, both father and mother feel liberated when children are launched. If a family has assumed that mothers do most of the accommodating for the sake of children during childrearing, it is mothers also who feel the greatest freedom and the greatest loss when children leave. In traditional families, that freedom often did not change what women did inside or outside the home. Today, however, this new freedom provides an opportunity for women to pursue their own interests or follow a dream they had set aside in order to raise their children. What women choose to do with their freedom is sometimes more than their husbands are prepared for.

> We moved to a new city after our youngest child finished high school. It was my new job that moved us. It was demanding and I loved it. More than that, I loved the feeling of freedom that I felt, especially after our daughter left for college. For the first time in my life, I did not feel confined by obligations or expectations to anyone at home. I could come and go as I wished. It was a heady time for me. My husband, however, had a hard time adjusting to my new sense of freedom.   (Beverly)

Beverly's discovery of new freedom is not uncommon for women who have felt confined by the responsibilities of childrearing. How to spend that new freedom is an even more complicated issue in a marriage that strives to be egalitarian. It is easier for both parents to limit their freedom *because* they have in common a commitment to the well-being of the children. When the needs of children are less and parenting responsibilities diminish, a wife and husband may need to discover new expressions of generativity or a shared cause to sustain marriage without children. That is one of the reasons we regard promising again as so necessary for the future of a marriage.

The relationship between parenting, leaving home, and promising again is increasingly complex. Part of the complexity has to do with adult children moving in and out of the home. In addition, there are cultural traditions that have become more visible in this society in which it is frequently expected that children will live at home until they marry. Economic factors have also affected the relationship between leaving home and promising again. Children cannot afford to leave home and married sons and daughters live with their parents because of financial necessity. There are also gender changes taking place. One can no longer assume that diminishing the active parent role will be stressful only for women. Both parents may welcome the freedom that comes when children leave home, even though their relationship may not be prepared for it. All of these changes add to the importance of promising again when the nest is emptying.

Critical Factors in Promising Again

When the process of promising again works well as the nest empties, couples find new freedom to reinvest in their relationship beyond the initial promise. Because there are alliances, wives and husbands "bump up against each other" more often. Fewer alliances to work with, plus greater freedom of choice, intensify the need to promise again at this moment in the history of a marriage. Promising again cannot be hurried. It takes time to revive love, heal memories, and negotiate new patterns of relating. Nonetheless, as children are being launched, there are critical factors that will impede or foster *creative fidelity* for the sake of their marriage.

A Child-Stabilized Marriage

One of the characteristics of promising again is the willingness to let go of the past. It is particularly difficult for parents to let go of the child whose role it has been to provide a buffer between parents for the sake of their marriage. Husbands and wives will look for ways to avoid meeting one another without children between them. It is equally difficult for the designated child to leave with the knowledge that the parents' marriage will be in jeopardy.

> When I left for college, I determined never to go home again to live, and I didn't. My sister Nancy was not so fortunate, however. She was needed at home to balance the family, and Nancy cooperated by getting sick in the middle of her first year in college. When my sister and I decided to marry in the same year, it was more change than the system could bear. My family literally split in two. This fragmentation intensified my father's depression. After many successful years in business, he was on the brink of financial disaster because of unwise investments. Two weeks before my sister's wedding, while I was still on my honeymoon, my father committed suicide. He had lost too much. And a good-enough family had been shattered by more losses at once than it could handle.   (Roxanne)

Roxanne's parents managed to stay together because Nancy had been willing to sacrifice her own future in order to keep them together. When Nancy decided to marry, however, the buffer between her parents was gone. Although Roxanne seems to be less emotionally involved in sustaining her parents' marriage, for both daughters to marry in one year was too much for a relationship already strained by the father's depression. When a home is suddenly vacated by one or more of its stabilizing occupants, even a good-enough family may be thrown off balance. A family's capacity to survive the necessary and predictable departures of children hinges on the strength of the marital bond or the ability of the couple to rebuild their relationship without the buffer of children.

Even if the child who keeps the family together leaves home, couples may delay facing their own life together by continuing to be overinvolved in the careers of their children. When the children are *really* settled becomes an expandable category. It may not be enough to get a job or an apartment. Parents sometimes continue to be actively involved in parenting their adult children until they are married, own a home, and have children of their own. Letting go of the parenting role as a primary activity of the marital pair is often a painful, but nonetheless crucial factor in enhancing the possibility of promising again.

Overlapping Crises: Personal and Marital

In some situations, the two tasks that couples need to accomplish when children leave become overlapping crises. Husbands and wives need to build a relationship in which parenting is not the focus. At the same time, each partner must find an enduring sense of personal meaning for the rest of life. Although this second task is more individual, it is worked out within our families, as well as in contexts of work and play. It has to do with the coincidental life-crisis that many people experience in the middle years of life. If a woman sets aside her dreams for a career for the sake of the children and the household, the end of the parenting role is both opportunity and challenge. For men, the issues may be more about finitude.

> We celebrated our twenty-fifth anniversary by taking our two children and their significant others to see *Les Miserables.* We had seats in the fourth row of Chicago Theatre. At the conclusion of the musical, when the father, Jean Valjean, sings a blessing to his daughter Cosette and her lover Mario, I began to sob uncontrollably. It did not take me long to connect my tears with hearing my father's voice on our wedding tape at breakfast that morning. There were many reasons for my sadness, but one of them was hearing a blessing that I never received from my father. (Herbert)

It is common for middle-aged fathers and mothers to deal with children leaving home, the sickness or death of parents, the unstable future of their children, and their own finitude at the same time. Herbert's grief was added to the celebration of an anniversary in a way common to human transitions. He cried for a blessing he had not received in the company of his children who also needed a blessing. Sometimes it is difficult for parents to give what they have never received. A middle-aged parent's identity search may cloud the ability to be empathic with young adult children who are struggling to discover their own sense of self.[6]

Remembering Too Well

Both remembering and forgetting are necessary in order to promise again. One of the most common factors that prevents couples from promising again is an unwillingness to forget old hurts and slights; to disregard old personality traits, to ignore the catalog of faults since redeemed, or to overlook the sadness that lingers concerning unfulfilled and unspoken expectations. Promising again is more likely to occur if both partners develop a shared remembrance for past good times and a shared amnesia for past wounds. Promising again is most difficult when one partner forgets and the other remembers and remembers and remembers. If there has been genuine reconciliation despite past hurts, amnesia is not necessary. When the healing of painful memories is mutual, they can be talked about, even laughed at.

It is always the case that the person with whom we must promise again is not exactly the same person we married, or at least not the one we *thought* we married. The basic features may be the same. The body contours are familiar. But people change as they grow older. It takes courage for husbands and wives to allow one another to change. We need to be free to let go of old images or past perceptions in order to acknowledge the changes that have occurred in each partner during the marriage. This is a kind of forgetting that is liberating.

The couple that promises again in marriage is both the same as and different than the couple who made their initial promises at the wedding. When recognition of the uniqueness of the other in marriage has been part of the relationship all along, this new moment of promising builds on enduring respect. This time, we surrender our vision of what we think our partner ought to become, in order to commit to the one to whom we are married. That opens up the future. We also need to let go of some memories from the past in order to be free to remember. That opens up the past.

The Sandwich Generation

Promising is an act of mutuality. Sometimes, however, a couple's energy and loyalty is divided between launching adult children and caring for aging parents. As a result, mutuality is in short supply. Adult children sometimes feel slighted because the attention of their parents is diverted away from the trauma of their launching by the needs of grandparents. When the needs of parents' parents dominate after children have been launched, the freedom that parents have waited for is short-lived. The responsibilities of caring for aging parents is a new limitation for one or both of the marital pair. Sometimes, however, the problem is with parents. Middle-aged daughters or sons who miss parenting their own children create needs in aging parents, or even infantilize them, in order to have someone to care for.

When parents must spend time and energy caring for elderly parents, as well as attend to the task of launching reluctant leavers into the adult world, there may not be enough time or energy to nurture the marital bond. What is sometimes referred to as "the sandwich generation" is a relatively new phenomenon. It is a consequence of the fact that people live longer so that sons and daughters in their fifties or sixties or seventies are still caring for their aging parents; and that young people who find it difficult to find work, or find work that does not support them in the manner to which they have become accustomed, are likely to return home to live. Not only is the freedom of parents tabled, but they are caught between the conflicting obligations of the generations. *Parent caregiving* is a major source of stress in family living. And the new freedom that parents look forward to after childrearing is often limited by new responsibilities for aging parents.

We are most acutely aware of the cycle of generations in this transitional moment. It is difficult for parents to grant adult status to their own children if one or both of the parents do not believe they have received it from their own parents. In the worst situations, parents withhold a blessing from their own children because they themselves have not been blessed. If middle-aged sons and daughters must wait to stand on the grave of a parent in order to declare their autonomy, their children who are leaving may have to wait for autonomy as well.

Balancing the Fundamental Paradoxes

The moment when the nest is emptying highlights the need to keep paradox alive in marriage in three ways. Each of these paradoxes is common to the life cycle of a family and have been major themes throughout this series on Family Living in Pastoral Perspective. In an earlier book in this series, *Becoming Married,* we noted that one of the central aspects of becoming married is the recognition of and respect for the uniqueness of the other in the relationship. Without the presence of children, husbands and wives have a new possibility to see one another directly and more deeply. Recognizing the uniqueness of the other and celebrating the community in marriage are both essential for successful promising again at any time.

Being Separate Together

The two great longings for humankind are to belong and to be separate. The family is a context that honors both: it celebrates autonomy and promotes human community. Being separate and being together is, in fact, the fundamental paradox of humanness. The capacity to be separate and to be together are therefore reciprocally related. Each needs the other. Families are likely to get into trouble when one side of that paradox is exaggerated at the expense of the other.

When the children leave, the freedom for separateness or the expectation of togetherness in marriage presses the question again. It is a crucial issue in promising again when the paradox is understood differently within the same marriage. Some people understand marriage to be two clearly separate people, with quite separate lives, who intentionally come together from time to time. Being separate is the norm. Being together is the choice. Others understand marriage as a unit in which togetherness is primary but people go out from that unity to do things separately in the world. The presence of children from the sexual union of these two people forms a common bond. As long as the children are home, couples are more likely to think of themselves as a unit. When children are launched, the paradox of being separate together must be reviewed to be sustained.

Continuity and Discontinuity

The balance between continuity and discontinuity in human life in general and family living in particular is another theme that has been constant throughout this series. *Promising again* presumes change and discontinuity. The greater the change, the greater the necessity for reviewing and renewing promises made when things were different. We assume that change continues to occur in a relationship because people continue to change as they grow older. When the changes that occur in a relationship are hardly noticeable, the need to promise again is blurred by the appearance of continuity. At least, the departure of children heralds a role change in the marriage that requires attention to the relationship.

Past and Future

Even when the changes in our lives seem radically discontinuous, there are hidden threads that hold together the tapestry of our lives. Although it is both possible and necessary for couples to promise again, the act of promising takes seriously the couple's shared life and common history that makes promising both difficult and necessary. The relationship between the past and the future is critical for understanding promising in or out of marriage. We cannot absolutize either the determining power of the past or the liberating power of the future, if we are to renew promises in the present.

There are two common myths about the past and the present that doom authentic promising again. One myth absolutizes the future and denies the past. *Let's move to Vermont and start over again.* That wish is based on the unrealistic assumption that the marital bond has no history. The second myth romanticizes the past and limits future change. *If only we could find our first love again.* This myth is based on the conviction that there is no future that has not been determined already by the past. The expectation is that the future will be fine if we can recover what was lost from the past. The promise of a future in which God makes things new is muffled by the desire to recover early romance. The human act of promising honors and limits the past and presumes that the future is both open and unknown.

Beyond the Emptying Nest

The primary moment for promising again occurs when children are being launched. There are, however, other anticipated moments of ordinary change that may destabilize the bond. When children are added is one such time; another is when retirement begins. Even when families satisfactorily navigate their way through the emptying nest transition, they face similar issues at the time of retirement. Couples need to promise again when retirement reconfigures life, providing new freedom and loss, more time for revitalized intimacy or renewed conflict, new opportunities and risks. The change may be more or less dramatic than when children are launched, depending on the character of the marriage. The old joke is true if the woman did not work outside the home. "I married him for better or for worse but not for lunch every day." Even if both partners in a marriage worked outside the home, the rhythm of the marriage changes when one or both retires. Because the balance of a relationship shifts at retirement, both partners need to learn new roles.

Work, like children, may serve to hold a marriage together. It may be the source of gratification, self-esteem, and social contact for both spouses. The marital bond may be chaotic or conflicted, negligent or cold, but the work context provides the social and emotional nutriments that the marriage does not. In such a marriage, freedom from work may strike terror in one or both partners. Depression and despair, dashed dreams of a continual vacation, and even divorce often accompany retirement in a work-stabilized marriage.

Couples who are prepared to promise again when retirement begins delight in new freedom and new opportunities for intimacy. People are often better prepared for retirement than they were for launching children. Preretirement programs have fostered a kind of *second-curve thinking* in which people are strongly urged to begin financial planning for this transition long before it occurs. There are emotional issues to attend to as well. In addition to greater freedom, alliances change again as people leave the workplace. Grandparenting often fills a void created by other losses. As with any other major transition in marriage, it will become a gift of joy if the couple is able to renew their *primary* promise in light of unavoidable changes.

Marks of Promising Again

When we face moments in which change overwhelms us or when we wonder whether we are able to be faithful, it is helpful to have some sense of what the process of promising again looks like when it is going well. What personal qualities or ways of responding to situations will enhance the possibility of promising again? And what are some marks or indications that it is happening? We do not intend to suggest a blueprint for promising again, because each situation is unique and requires certain responses more than others. We have, however, put the following qualities in the verb form again to emphasize the awareness that promising is an ongoing process. Each of these dynamics reflects dimensions of faithful living consistent with the Christian tradition.

1. *Compromising.* The ability to compromise is the heart of promising again. Theologian Daniel Day Williams has identified the passion of "being conformed to another" (promise with) as an essential component in committed relationships that endure.[7] We are *formed* and *re-formed* as we are *conformed* to one another in the act of promising together. Yet we cannot actualize all the potential we have. Compromise is another way through paradox. Handy asserts that, "We have no chance of managing the paradoxes if we are not prepared to give up something, if we are not willing to bet on the future, and if we cannot find it in ourselves to take a risk with people."[8] Compromising is necessary because the activity of promising again occurs in the midst of competing interests and human limits. Marriage demands that both partners are willing to meet each other halfway. Judith Wallerstein adds this sober caution, "Before marrying, couples should also beware: some compromises demand too much; the price can be too high. No one should give away his or her heart's desire."[9] This is another way of expressing what we have identified as *creative fidelity.*

2. *Letting Go.* Every recommitment in human relationships involves several forms of surrendering or letting go. We relinquish individual images of who we thought we would be and leave behind familiar ways of being or thinking about ourselves when we decide to renew a promise for the sake of a new future. We grieve for what was or what might have been, for the familiar and the known, for the selves we were, and for who we thought we were. When we promise again we also surrender our vision of what a marriage or what a spouse should be. Marriage may be less than we thought it would be or we hoped it would be. It may also be much more than we imagined or hoped for. Letting go is the way we put closure on the past. We cannot promise again or marry again until we let go of old memories, old hurts and offenses, or old images of ourselves and how we will keep our promises. Letting go is an act of closure, but it is not necessarily termination. When we confuse closure and termination, we presume that the only way to close the door on a painful dimension of our life is to terminate it altogether.

3. *Trusting.* We cannot know in advance the outcome of any

promise we make. In that sense, making any promise is a wager on the future that takes courage as well as trust. At the heart of trusting is the assurance that each one will keep his or her promises. Our disappointments in relationships make it more difficult to trust. Because we have been discouraged by our own fickleness and hurt by the faithlessness of others, we approach with fear and trepidation the need to promise again. And the more we have been wounded or violated in relationships, the harder it becomes to trust. We know the risks. It takes courage and trust to try again to recommit ourselves. The more we experience broken promises in human communities, the more difficult and more necessary it is to remember God's steadfastness.

4. *Remembering and Forgetting.* In order to see someone we love in a new way, we need to let go of old perceptions. At the same time, paradoxically, our promising again is based on the remembrance of who we are and what we believe in. We cannot find the thread of continuity in the midst of change or the path of fidelity marked out by our promises unless we remember both who we are and whose we are. We rehearse the initial promise in order to transform it. There are also occasions when it is more important to forget than to remember. We have to forget petty grievances, unintended slights, even major disappointments in order to create space for new possibilities of fidelity. If we remember without forgetting, we hold on to the past in a way that inhibits promising again. If we forget the past, however, the discontinuity will be too great and we may overlook past hurts that must be healed. Promising again is hollow in its center unless it includes both remembering and forgetting.

5. *Forgiving.* It is forgiveness that makes our most profound commitments sustainable. Because we are limited creatures, our original promising is never perfect. We are not who we hoped to be, and we regularly discover that others are not who we thought them to be. We frequently fail to keep our promises. We cannot see our commitments through without the offer of forgiveness at critical moments on the marital journey. It is the experience of forgiveness and reconciliation that shows us the way through to fidelity when we come up against our incapacities, our limits, or our failures.

> When Becky and I were married, she was already pregnant. Becky was terrified to tell my parents but I was not. They responded as I expected. They loved Becky and they could see that Becky loved me. That was enough for them. My grandma wasn't so easy, however. Eventually, though, she too accepted

Becky with reservation when her first great-grandchild was born. Our wedding was the best, pregnancy and all. My parents have a way of embracing the good in every situation. Above all else, I want my new family to be like that.   (Kent)

The story of Kent and Becky is about the reciprocal relationship between forgiveness and trust. There is no forgiveness without trust, yet learning to trust another again presumes repentance. Promising again means learning to say "I'm sorry." The kind of forgiveness that makes it possible to promise again is not a hasty truce, however. It will need to include knowing when saying "I'm sorry" is not enough.

6. *Being Vulnerable.* Promising again is fraught with the possibilities of disappointment and hurt. Even when two people determine jointly and in good faith to enter into a process of renewal, it is impossible to anticipate the outcome. Neither can one anticipate all the hurtful memories that may be recalled or the painful differences that might be discovered. Promising again is a process that requires a willingness to be vulnerable in the literal sense of "susceptible to being wounded." When a couple willingly determines to reconsider and renew their promise, each becomes vulnerable. That is the risk of promising again. It is also the mark of a relationship in which partners have learned how to be intimate.

7. *Waiting.* Waiting is necessary in order to promise again for two reasons. The human soul does not hurry. The same must be said about the soul of a marriage. Whenever we hurry compromise or forgiveness, we undermine the possibility of the renewal of the covenants that sustain human living in and out of family. We need to allow time and space for the promise to grow and become seasoned. No promise is fulfilled in an instant. Waiting is also necessary because it means that we approach the task of promising again with expectation. We wait in hope. And when we wait, we live in the expectation that promising again is possible. This posture of waiting as part of promising again requires acts of creative imagination, good humor, patience, and some courage. The opportunity to renew a promise often comes at times and in ways we never imagined or anticipated. This experience of the unexpected fulfillment of the promise is at the heart of our religious heritage. We need courage to be free to be surprised.

8. *Signs that Promising Again Is Working.* When the process of promising again is working well, some of the following marks are likely to be present.

—Parents reconnect with each other when their children are too busy making new friendships and finding new love of their own to be available for conversation or even family gatherings.

—Parents know that something has changed when their adult children are slightly embarrassed, delighted, or dismayed that their parents are not at home as predictably as they used to be.

—Brothers and sisters turn toward one another and form a natural grouping according to the generations.

—When the adult child whose job it has been to keep parents together complains about being excluded from the plans or the confidence of parents.

—When parents and adult children become friends. This is especially important if adult children come back to live with their parents.

—When couples begin to plan trips together, think about retirement, or remodel their house.

Promising again, like making the initial promise, is an intentional act—a recommitment to a common future that is like hope thrown ahead. It is an act of creative fidelity representing a fidelity to the self we have promised to be within the communities we are committed to sustain. When promising again occurs at the moment the nest is emptying, it may require painful negotiation, deliberate compromising, a balance between forgetting and remembering, and hopeful waiting. Sometimes we discover in retrospect that the process of promising again has been going on without our intention.

Rituals that Enhance Promising Again

The initial promise of marriage was a public act that occurred in the context of ritual. The process of promising again is also strengthened when it can be ritualized in a public setting. Within the Roman Catholic tradition, it is common for couples to mark twenty-five or fifty years of marriage with a eucharistic liturgy. It is usually a public ritual that includes one or more couples who celebrate a significant anniversary of marriage with a liturgy in the parish church or in their home. Although there is no parallel ritualistic practice within the Protestant tradition, couples often develop a prayer ritual to include as part of a wedding anniversary party. It is public in the sense that family and friends are often present for the party, but it is not connected explicitly to a faith community.

Within the Roman Catholic tradition, this anniversary ritual of remembering and blessing occurs within the context of the Eucharist. The "Blessing within Mass on the Anniversary of Marriage" will include (1) restating or reaffirming the first vow, (2) a blessing of rings (that may or may not be the original rings), (3) general intercessions for the couple and all married persons, and (4) a particular blessing for the couple. This framework could be used in any religious setting or tradition. In the Roman Catholic liturgies, the prayers invite both the couple and the congregation to remember with gratitude the gifts of God's grace that have "preserved the union between them." The couple is also invited to "be mindful of the covenant of love they pledged to each other . . . and never fail in fidelity."[10] The focus of the prayers, however, is more on keeping the initial promise than promising again.

Marking the twenty-fifth or the fiftieth year of marriage is a recognition of its enduring character. It is also a way of celebrating the importance of permanency in the sacramental understanding of marriage. The marital pair are honored quite independent of where their family is in the life-cycle transitions. The emphasis usually is on continuity rather than change. One of the negative consequences of this emphasis on chronology only is that joyless marriages, in which one or both partners are starving emotionally, are celebrated for their durability.

Anniversaries are times of remembering and promising again in order to discover the possibility of seeing new meaning in the past as it unfolds in the present. As Farley has observed, anniversaries "are not just moments to recall historical events and times. They hold an accumulated meaning, the meaning of what life within this committed relationship has become. They offer the possibilities of sorting out, letting go, or ratifying."[11] It is important, therefore, that the prayers and blessings at a ritual honoring a marriage not only recognize the inevitable joys and struggles of life but celebrate new promises that have come from the discovery of new gifts in one another and in the relationship.

Sometimes, coincidentally, the anniversary year marks the life-cycle transition as well. Children plan the event as a sign of their new status in the family. New family members are incorporated into the system. Thus it becomes a double ceremony that celebrates launching as well as marrying again. Couples who marry and postpone having children are more likely to celebrate their twenty-fifth anniversary of marriage before the nest is emptying. The advantage of that process is that there are then two natural times for couples to recommit to each other and to the marriage: the silver anniversary and launching children.

The aim of this chapter has been to explore the need for promising again before, during, and after the time of launching young adult children. There is a delicate reciprocity between leaving home or launching and promising again. When children are launched, parents have time and energy to promise again. And when parents are clear about their desire to renew the marital bond, it is easier for adult children to leave home. Although this is the most predictable time when couples must reaffirm their commitment to each other, it is not the only time. There are a variety of unexpected moments in a family's life when changes within or without the system necessitate review and renewal of the marital bond. Next we will consider those times of unexpected change when promising again is also necessary for the survival of a marriage.

3

WHEN THE
UNEXPECTED OCCURS

MARRIAGES CHANGE over time because people and circumstances change. Some of those transitions, such as emptying the nest, are predictable consequences of the development of each member, or the growth of the family as a whole. Other stress is unexpected. Forces from outside the system or choices from inside the family create stress and demand some fundamental changes. Any change poses a crisis if the stress evoked by the change exceeds the family's ability to adapt to that change. Because change is inevitable, *marriage is always a work in progress.*

Adaptability is a family's capacity to adjust its roles, rules, relationships, behaviors, and beliefs in response to a change from outside the family and changing needs or demands from within. Family therapist and researcher David Olson has defined adaptability as "the ability of a marital or family system to change its power structure, role relationships, and relationship rules in response to situational and developmental stress."[1]

The adaptability of the couple is particularly stretched by the "slings and arrows of outrageous fortune" coming from outside the family. Some catastrophic events are traumatic even for the strongest families, but even common stress may produce a family crisis if the resources for coping are not adequate. The vitality of a marital bond may also be threatened by choices made by one or both of the partners. Whatever the source of the change that creates instability in the marital bond, we believe that the response is the same: the relationship must be renegotiated and renewed to be maintained.

We planned to have only two children. Both my husband Jack and I were concerned about population growth. When our youngest child was eleven, I became pregnant again. The timing could not have been worse. I had just returned to work at an advertising firm where I had worked before the children were born. Jack wanted me to have an abortion but I refused. We tried to find a compromise, but finally Jack left.

(Rosemary)

Most of our sixteen years of marriage had seemed like a steady upward climb. We had our own home and enough money to provide for our children without worry. When the company I worked for was sold, I was out of work and out of sorts for more than two years. Eventually, we learned to live with less money and more conflict. (Barry)

Carter and I decided shortly after Matthew was born developmentally disabled that we would care for him at home as long as we could. When Matthew was eleven, however, we had to put him in an institution because he was too strong for us to manage. It was not until he was gone that we realized how much of our life as a couple and a family had been shaped by his presence. (Isabel)

Until we decided to have children, I did not think about my marriage as a permanent thing. I would often tell Steve that we could get a divorce if things didn't work out. When we decided to have a child, it felt like my commitment to Steve had to be permanent in a new way. (Carly)

Betty regularly ran early in the morning by a lake in the city where we live. I thought it was unwise and unsafe, but she persisted. She would not allow her life to be governed by fear. Then she was raped one morning. . . . I knew it was not her fault, but our relationship never recovered from that tragedy.

(Raymond)

I had seen less and less of Jeffrey over the last several years. He was a career officer in the Air Force and every promotion seemed to make him work harder. If it had not been for our six children, I would have left long ago. When he volunteered for deployment in Egypt, I thought seriously of divorce. When he was in Egypt, he lost our wedding ring. Jeffrey felt so badly about losing the ring that he insisted we have a church ceremony to bless his new ring. I was a little annoyed that he seemed to worry more about losing a ring than losing his family. Nonetheless, it was the beginning of a new marriage and the renewal of our life together. (Carol Anne)

As long as I can remember, my mother had never been pleased with anything I said or did. Whenever I moved toward even a little self-esteem, she would find a way to knock me down. My husband would prop me up after one of mother's blasts. I was forty-three when my mother died. Without her criticism, I discovered my voice, found new gifts, and claimed my autonomy. It was a time of liberation. I was not prepared for my husband's reaction, however. Overnight he became less supportive and more critical. (Clarise)

Melanie and I had a brief, intense courtship. Because both of us had been married before, there were many things we needed to tell each other. After we had been married for almost ten years, she withdrew sexually. When I pressed for a reason, Melanie told me that her father had sexually abused her until she was fourteen. Although I understood her pain, I could not live with her sexual distance from me. (Larry)

After we were married, we lived in a trailer court near a river. During a spring flood, we lost everything we owned. We had been warned about the possibility of a flood, but we had not been warned about its consequences. Our marriage was almost washed away with the mementos from our wedding.

(Peggy)

Each of the above stories describes a change that significantly altered the balance of a marriage. Every change in family living is potentially disruptive. However, some of the changes cited above were permanently damaging because more flexibility or intimacy or communication was required than the family could effect or endure. People who want their marriage to remain as it began may leave it rather than accept the changes that occur unavoidably over time. When a couple anticipates change as a norm for family living, they are better prepared for the transitions and crises that inevitably occur throughout the life cycle of a family.

We began this chapter with a chronicle of crises in order to expand our awareness of the need to promise again. Family therapist Frank S. Pittman III observes that "marriage and change may seem to be in conflict, and at times they are incompatible, but if the changes and the marriage are both understood they usually can be accommodated."[2] Promising again in marriage begins with acknowledging the change that has prompted a crisis in the relationship. This crisis usually involves a challenge at the level of *secondary promise*. The permanence of our loyalty, the exclusivity of our commitment, or the enduring character of recognition has been challenged by a crisis. When we can identify the crisis, we have a chance to modify expectations or alter patterns of interaction in order to restore balance and strengthen the marital bond. For that reason, *intentionality* is not simply a wedding prerequisite; it is an ongoing necessity in marriage.

Becoming Married and Promising Again

Becoming married is a lifelong process. In that sense, making a distinction between becoming married and promising again is arbitrary. After the initial promise to wed, husband and wife continue committing to each other and to the marriage as they make decisions and discover new dimensions of their relationship. Becoming and staying married is a lifelong process of unnoticed commitments and intentional recommitment. Covenants must be renewed in order to be kept.

At the beginning of every marriage there is a period of time when bonding or joining is the couple's primary emotional work. It is not always clear, however, when this focused time of becoming married is completed so that couples can or should say "Now we are married." Because many changes in a marital relationship are gradual, couples may not know that they have become married until the bond is later challenged by a crisis. They discover in retrospect that something has changed about their life together. Or they may have to make a decision that challenges their commitment to one another and the marriage.

> Gary and I had known each other for seven years and we had been married for three years when he was offered a teaching position in another state. In order to move with him, I would have had to give up a teaching position I loved and that promised long-term security. I had never been so aware of being married. I also discovered that Gary felt that he had made

> an emotional commitment to the marriage before I had. Gary
> turned down the job offer, but every decision we have made
> since then begins with a rehearsal of that moment.   (Sara)

Sara's awareness of being married corresponded with a complex choice she and Gary had to make. It was a defining moment in their process of becoming married. Individuals within a marriage, as this story suggests, may experience the timetable of that process differently. For Sara, the defining moment of becoming married occurred when they had to decide about the job offer that would have required her to give up a permanent teaching position. Sara remembered that moment because she knew that their relationship was forever complicated and changed by the decision. The process of promising again often generates anxiety for people like Gary and Sara because they must revisit a prior decision that one or both of them may choose to unmake. Promising again, as we use it here, begins whenever the process of becoming married ends.

This chapter is about the unexpected and extraordinary crises that occur *after* the initial period of intense bonding. We distinguish here between becoming married and promising again only to emphasize the necessity of recommitment when the changes in a relationship or its context are significant enough to threaten its stability. Whether a change becomes a destabilizing crisis for a couple depends on when it occurs in the family's history, the intensity or complexity of the change, what coping resources are available from the system, the meaning a family attaches to the change, and the well-being of the marriage at the time of the crisis.

Cultural, ethnic, and economic factors modify the resources available to couples for responding to a crisis. There are many factors that affect a couple's capability to respond constructively to a crisis. If a couple has lived through a number of crises, they develop a confidence in their capacity to cope with stress that families who have not previously endured stress may not have. The developmental tasks of family members may overlap with an unexpected crisis and either multiply the stress or create a conflict of needs. Or the crisis may fall so far outside the family's ordinary range of functioning that it does not have accessible modes for coping.

The kinds of unexpected crises that families may face throughout the life cycle are many and diverse, but can be organized into four broad categories—natural or human-made disaster, physical loss, socioeconomic stress, and psychological or spiritual change. Included in these four categories are stresses that may challenge a family's capacity to adapt in particular ways, illustrating again the major characteristics of the process of promising again.

The Chaos of Disasters

A natural disaster, such as a hurricane, tornado, flood, fire, or earthquake often causes unspeakable human agony. In our time, there is also the threat of such disasters as the meltdown of a nuclear reactor, war, or terrorism that are the consequence of either human error or malice. A disaster is a sudden, calamitous event that causes property damage and human hardship, as well as resulting in death and destruction, homelessness and long-term suffering, economic loss, and social disruption. Some disasters strike whole communities, and the family may be strengthened by sharing resources and responses with many others. Other disasters may hit only a single family, and the family's loss becomes uniquely its own.

When a family faces a catastrophe together, there is a bond created by a shared experience that transcends previous divisions in the system. The mutuality that is a significant dimension of promising again happens naturally. At the same time, family routines are disrupted. Rules, roles, and responsibilities need to shift. Nothing is as it was before, and yet everything is the same. A disaster also challenges a family's coping resources. It is generally agreed that families are best able to cope with disaster-caused stresses if they have adapted successfully to other life crises.[3]

> We were at a neighbor's house when we heard the fire truck drive down our street. By the time we got there, our whole house was in flames. I have never felt so helpless. We lost everything we owned, every memento of our marriage, every letter we had ever received, and a room full of paintings we had bought from friends who were artists. Our three daughters were devastated. They did not sleep through the night for months afterward because we had learned that the fire had been set by someone I had recently fired from the company. My wife felt victimized. She wanted to talk about the fire all the time. My response was to firm up the security and eliminate every window of vulnerability but forget the fire.   (Richard)

When families experience disaster they are left with a heightened sense of vulnerability. Parents and children alike are made painfully aware that the worst in life *can* happen to them. Parents intuitively sense that they must be strong (that is, not anxious) for the sake of the children. Yet studies show that when parental fears are unrecognized or denied, the child's fears are heightened, and parents are less able to effectively deal with the child's anxieties.[4] When parents can share their own fears, children do not feel a need to hide theirs. Therefore, a family in which there is honest expression of fear will be more likely to endure the helplessness that follows a natural disaster.

A disaster also evokes a heightened sense of discontinuity for both individuals and families. Richard's family lost everything except their lives and their commitment to one another. In response to such total and discontinuous loss, it is important for families to find continuity in the solidarity of family love and the dependability of family roles. *Promising again when a disaster occurs presumes a willingness to acknowledge human vulnerability*. Richard's protective life style did not prepare the family for the possibility of a disaster. Neither did his desire to eliminate all "windows of vulnerability" after the fire diminish the fears of his wife and daughters.

Families that are shut off from their environment also presume to be invulnerable to outside forces. It is as though the safety of the family depends on a fierce protection that is intent on keeping evil outside. In order to renew the bonds of marriage and reweave the tapestry of a family after a disaster, each member needs to practice *creative worrying* in order to foster a way of living that willingly looks at human vulnerability and is therefore not surprised by disaster when it occurs. In addition to being vulnerable with one another, promising again after a natural disaster may mean letting go of an old vision of the world. A harder task for Richard and his family will be to revision the world after the fire in a way that takes into account the possibility of disasters and unexpected suffering without paralyzing fear.

Physical Losses: Death, Infertility, and Illness

Families confront changes they would never have chosen. Illness enters the family; death takes a family member at a young age; hope for bearing children is never realized. Physical losses and handicaps change the rules of family living and call for promising again when the hoped-for life together runs headlong into life as it is. We look here at three losses that are grounded in our mortality. Each illustrates the need for recognizing human finitude as an occasion for promising again.

Losses in the family regularly make our acceptance of life's limits personal, unavoidable, and painful.

The Death of a Child

The death of a child is often described as the worst tragedy a family can imagine. Before the turn of this century, however, it was almost an expected occurrence. In many parts of the world, including the United States, infant mortality is still much too high. Nonetheless, most parents expect their children to outlive them. When a child dies, it is experienced as a violation of the natural order. It is also experienced by some parents as a sign that they have failed in their function to protect their children from the ravages of death. As a result, it is not surprising that grieving parents are preoccupied about the circumstances of the death in order to restore their sense of competence.[5]

Promising again after there has been a death in the family depends on the family's willingness to acknowledge the reality of the loss and to share the grief. This is never easy. Even the strongest marital bond is heavily burdened by the task of grieving the death of a child. Studies have shown that the risk of marital breakup rises significantly after the death of a child.[6] Religious resources may provide comfort for parents facing the death of a child. Even so, it is crucial that parents support each other when a child dies. If the reality of the loss is denied, the grief cannot be shared. If the grief cannot be shared, it becomes a serious barrier in the relationship. This is another instance in which being vulnerable is a prerequisite for promising again.

> The story of the disintegration of a family after the death of a child is graphically told in the novel *Ordinary People* by Judith Guest. Buck, the oldest son of Calvin and Beth Jarrett, has drowned. The younger brother, Conrad, carries the family's pain for that loss. Beth insists that nothing be changed in Buck's room or in any other aspect of her life. Conrad eventually gets better, but his parents marriage disintegrates. At one point, before their separation, Cal is aware that a widening and threatening fault is growing slowly between him and Beth. Around that time, he has the following rambling thoughts on grief: "A family turns inward toward itself in grief, it does not go in separate directions, pulling itself apart. Like hell it doesn't. Grief is ugly. It is isolating. It is not something to be shared with others, it is something to be afraid of, to get rid of, and fast."[7]
>
> It was the inability to deal with their grief together that caused the Jarrett family to disintegrate.

The grief over the death of a child like Buck is disruptive for a couple if it cannot be shared. When fathers and mothers are not available to one another, grief is hidden and the experience of vulnerability is covered over by a need to restore a sense of parental competence. "The death of a child can also leave couples profoundly estranged as they retreat into private and often discordant grief experiences."[8] When couples have not practiced sharing such deep emotions as grief, it will be difficult for them to renew their promises when a child dies.

If the growth of a parent's self is too closely linked to the child who has died, the death may also threaten the marital bond if the parent's self-image is damaged. "The more significant the child is to the parent's own sense of well-being or sense of self, the greater is the degree of family disruption after the death of that child."[9] Children often become highly significant to a parent when there is conflict in the marriage. Such parents must find ways to reclaim their own value as individuals — apart from the child — before it is possible to promise again. If the deceased child has been a buffer between parents, the couple must learn to relate to each other in new ways while they are grieving. *Learning to grieve together is a necessary first step in promising again after the death of a child.*

When a Parent Dies

The death of a parent can have a profound impact on middle-aged sons and daughters, which may, in turn, affect the equilibrium of a marital bond. When the last parent dies, middle-aged daughters and sons are suddenly more aware that the buffer is gone and death is closer. For those who have been evading the issue of finitude, however, the death of either parent is an unavoidable reminder that all of us need to come to terms with the limits placed on our lives.

The death of a parent also disrupts our sense of belonging. Middle-aged children become orphans, making their family of choice their only home. As a result, we may expect more from our children or be more critical of a spouse because it is the only family we have. Sometimes, middle-aged sons and daughters find new personal authority when a parent dies. When that discovery of autonomy occurs, the balance in a marriage may be changed dramatically if one spouse becomes more assertive. All of this is to say that marriages of middle-aged persons are potentially vulnerable when a parent dies.

> Two days after the wedding, my husband's father died. Obviously, we cut short our honeymoon in order to return for the funeral. At Oliver's insistence, we never spoke of his father again. As our three children grew older and more curious, I had to contrive excuses why they could not ask about their grandfather. My sister-in-law, who lived next door to us, was my lifeline throughout those early years. When she drowned suddenly in a canoe accident, I was bereft. Because I could not store any more grief, I felt I had to leave Oliver in order to live.
>
> (June)

Sometimes, any new loss can unstick old grief in ways that disrupt what is a fragile peace. June's story is about buried grief. After the death of Oliver's father, the family's equilibrium became inflexible. After the sudden and tragic death of her sister-in-law, that fixed family equilibrium was no longer tolerable to June. Family therapist Norman Paul demonstrates persuasively that marriages are often troubled when grief must be buried.[10] Sometimes the grief may be several generations old and in order to keep it hidden, the family must maintain patterns of interaction that make it difficult to express emotions, tell stories, or remember the past. *Learning how to grieve is a prelude to promising again.* For that reason, it may be said that families that grieve together, stay together.

The Problem of Infertility

Infertility is generally understood as the inability to become pregnant after one year of regular sexual intercourse without the use of any form of contraception. According to this definition, one in every five couples experience infertility at some time during a marriage. About two-thirds of those couples are able to conceive with medical assistance. Even so, it is an experience of invisible loss, evoking grief that often remains hidden because infertility is a taboo subject.[11] Because the grief is private, the pain is intensified and the stress on the marital bond is increased.

> We both always wanted children. I was raised in a large family, and even with the struggles to make ends meet and the crowded bathrooms, we had a strong family. We still get together for family reunions, and we practically take over the small town where we grew up. Bill's family was smaller, but they were close too. When I didn't get pregnant right away, we figured we were both just too anxious. We tried vacations so

we could both get away from the pressures of work. We finally went to a doctor, had all the diagnostic tests, even tried in vitro fertilization. Nothing worked. I could see Bill getting more and more depressed; he started spending even more time at work. I started avoiding family reunions because everybody kept asking me when we were going to have our own family. I guess Bill and I never could get past our personal hurts on the issue. We tried to talk about it, but we got nowhere. We started drifting farther and farther apart. (Charlotte)

Charlotte's story is a common one. It is not surprising that even stable marriages struggle under the pressures of infertility. Stress on the couple is likely in at least four areas.

1. *Sexual intercourse may become more focused on technique than on affection.* Sex according to the thermometer and the calendar easily becomes a production without passion. It is no longer a private, intimate moment, because the details are frequently discussed with a physician. Moreover, the process of trying to conceive is an emotional roller coaster of hope and failure. The longer the quest for a baby continues the greater possibility for distortion in the marital bond.

2. *The inability to conceive changes the expectations of a marriage.* Infertility means something different for each partner in the relationship. For some the loss centers around chances to carry on family name and heritage, the loss of chances for creativity, or the loss of sharing with another in love in creating life. For others the loss involves the chance to replicate oneself, or even to produce someone superior to yourself. For many there is a potential threat to masculinity or femininity or a fear of losing self-esteem and status in the community. For some there is a profound sense of shame, of not belonging in a family-focused world. When those dreams are private instead of shared, the grief is secret as well. And secret grief gnaws away at the partnership that is being formed in the marriage.

3. *Husbands and wives experience the crisis of infertility in different ways.* Even when the emotions are the same, women and men process them differently. Because each person is preoccupied with his or her own feelings, empathy for the other is difficult. Two persons seldom grieve the same way. This often causes partners to withdraw from each other. The grief is similar to the grief families have when a child dies or when there is a stillbirth or miscarriage.

4. *Because we want to know why things have happened—what their causes are—husbands and wives may be tempted to blame one an-*

other for the infertility, or to blame themselves. The extensive diagnostic procedures many couples endure to have children are geared toward discovering the causes of the problem, and either partner may feel shame or anger at the results of the testing—often in spite of an intellectual awareness that such feelings aren't rational. Such blaming, whether conscious or unconscious, can also lead to hiddenness, distance, and damage to the marriage. Infertility, like the loss due to miscarriage or the death of a child, hurts profoundly because it takes from us an experience that is intensely human—the experience of procreation.

In the face of infertility, promising again involves three distinct stages: grieving together for the children (and the family) who are not to be, re-creating the marriage in light of the certainty of infertility, and claiming new ways to invest in the next generation. Openness in grieving together is an opportunity for couples to develop intimate ways of joining each other around the difficult issues in life, thus creating a deeper bond. Dealing openly with this loss lays the groundwork for future losses the couple may have to face.

Building together new images of family, unique to this couple under these circumstances, opens new paths to the future and a growing sense of freedom in those choices. Exploring multiple ways to invest in the next generation, such as through adoption or foster care, involvement in church and community agencies that care for the young, or advocacy for disadvantaged groups and for the environment, gives expression to the couple's generativity in ways that go far beyond substitutions for children. They may, in fact, provide for the infertile couple a distinctive contribution to the community and a place in the world.

Illness in the Family

The sudden or even chronic illness of a spouse or child or parent creates a change that often destabilizes a marital relationship. It demands attention, requires sacrifice, diverts emotional energy, limits our freedom, diminishes or redirects financial resources, and challenges the loyalty of the marital pair to each other. The new patterns of marital interaction created by the crisis of illness frequently continue even after the illness subsides. Husbands and wives need to promise again when there is an illness in the family, because the balance in their relationship is permanently altered.

> One month before we were to celebrate our twenty-fifth wedding anniversary, my husband had a serious stroke. It was our

first real crisis. We had attained the "American Dream," with three children educated in private schools, a large home in the country, financial security, and a church we loved. Karl's stroke came at age forty-nine, shortly after he had begun a new professional career as a certified financial planner and just after my decision to return to school. When Karl began treatment, I found it hard to watch him struggle to place large wooden pegs in large holes. The full reality of his illness set in when he came home. He was impotent and angry. The stroke seemed to exaggerate his worst qualities. He was not the same person I married. And I was not the same person I thought I would be in a crisis.

I did not know if I could survive the changes in our life resulting from his illness. It was frightening for me even to think I would not keep my marriage vow to love Karl in sickness and in health. I did not share my struggle with him; he was fighting for his life. I remember thinking I had to choose to remarry Karl before I knew how the illness would turn out. It was a private decision, however, that Karl still does not know I made.

(Deborah)

The promise to love and cherish someone in sickness and health is usually made with little awareness of its consequences. The wedding is a time to minimize blemishes or overlook faults, but it is also a time to deny finitude. We promise without limits. It is understandable that we do not anticipate chronic illness, cancer, Alzheimer's disease, crippling arthritis, stroke, lingering depression, or disfiguring accidents when we make our wedding vows. For that reason, Deborah had it right. She needed to promise again because Karl was not the man she had married twenty-five years earlier. Her promise was not the same, because she had changed as well. Unfortunately, however, it was a private act. Deborah's recommitment to the marriage remained her burden—it was not an experience of mutuality shared with her husband.

Acute illness in the family often effects a sudden crisis that requires the rapid mobilization of coping resources. John Rolland, M.D., who has written widely about illness in the family, concludes: "Families that are able to tolerate highly charged affective states, exchange clearly defined roles flexibly, solve problems efficiently, and use outside resources will have an advantage in managing acute-onset illness."[12] When the onset of the illness is more gradual, the family has more time to gather resources, redistribute roles, and reorganize patterns of interaction. Illness that is episodic in its occurrence demands the most family flexibility, because it creates an atmosphere of permanent uncertainty.

Our focus here is on the impact of illness on the marital bond. It is impossible to consider in this brief space the varieties of illness that occur in families. Neither can we explore all the strategies necessary for coping with a family illness. *When* an illness occurs in the life cycle is another variable that determines the effectiveness of a family's response. For example, if the onset of illness in a family coincides with the leaving-home process of one member, the separation may be threatened, temporarily or permanently, because of family needs or because of the role of the one leaving. We need to assess the family's strengths and vulnerabilities in order to anticipate impending crises and to enhance appropriate adaptation at each transition in the development of an illness.

When the Illness Is Chronic

The ongoing task of the family is to provide a framework of freedom that supports the growth of each member while, at the same time, attending to the needs of the whole. That is what we have called *creative fidelity*. When an illness is incapacitating, that freedom is limited. A severely disabled child in a family, for instance, means that *everyone* is a little incapacitated. The husband of a woman who is agoraphobic needs to accept limits to his mobility if he is to continue the promise in the face of sickness. In every instance of incapacitating illness, it is crucial that sacrifice be justly distributed so that caring for the sick person does not permanently hinder the growth of any individual member of the family.

> I watched the woman I knew and loved as my mother vanish before my eyes—but it took six years for her to die. One day she wandered out of her home into the middle of the street, yelling and flailing at people who tried to help her. We knew then that she could not live alone. My sisters wanted to put her in a nursing home, but I could not do it. They said she had Alzheimer's. Even so, she was still my mother and I loved her. My wife and I had saved money to travel when I retired. With my wife's agreement, I used our travel money to get help when we needed it. We only put mother in a facility during the last three months of her life. Otherwise, she never left our house for six years. For me, the hardest thing was changing her diapers. She had been a proud and proper woman all her life.

> They call Alzheimer's the long good-bye. I said good-bye to my
> mother so many times, even after she no longer knew me. It
> was awful. (Tony)

Not everyone can, or should, make the choice that Tony made. For Tony, life was fundamentally altered for six years because of the presence of his mother. It was something both Tony and his wife had to agree on. People live longer. For that reason, adult children need to be prepared to care for elderly parents for a longer time. More and more couples must decide how to care for an elderly parent with an incapacitating disease. It is emotionally costly to care for a parent with Alzheimer's disease. Deciding to take care of Tony's mother in the home was an act of promising again for Tony and his wife. The promise first made in the abstract to love "in sickness and in health" became concrete. Now the promise was expanded to include Tony's mother.

What makes the decision of Tony and his wife so remarkable is that they willingly accepted the limits to their freedom that would be the consequence of his mother's presence in their home for six years. Couples first learn about limits to freedom when children are added to a family. Caring for a parent with an incapacitating disease such as Alzheimer's limits the freedom of a couple even more radically than the addition of children. Often the true victims are the family or the primary caregivers. Caregivers are themselves vulnerable to fatigue, frustration, and anger.

The presence of chronic illness in the family intensifies our need to understand promising as a continual activity. Whereas the illness may cause a deterioration in the person and increased need for care, chronic illness requires continual promising because the change is not about growth that presents new challenges to a relationship but about decline that makes the need for enduring bonds primary. It is a time for keeping promises, as well as for promising again.

Promising again when physical limitations have left their permanent marks calls for compromise. Each partner's interests must be renegotiated when death, illness, or infertility enters a family. Because the stress of grief and coping with illness frays our emotions, we are likely to respond to each other in ways for which we must later say "I'm sorry." Couples may need to compromise their own dreams and interests in the face of the new realities that illness brings. Confronting the realities of our mortality and finitude is a painful and unmistakable reminder of the finite human context in which all our promising occurs.

Social or Economic Stress

Changes in the outer world also influence events within the individual and the immediate family environment. Economic recessions, "right-sizing," firing, and layoffs strike families across the socioeconomic spectrum. The shock and displacement that families experience damage them both financially and emotionally as anxiety rises, self-esteem is threatened, and chaotic emotions erupt. In addition to the surprise stresses, the "mundane extreme environmental stress" on poor or minority families that results from economic inequality, poor education, poor health care, inadequate housing, and other factors generates a crisis that is more than most families can bear. "Unemployment is related to family instability and family functioning in the areas of marital power, family violence, spending behavior, division of labor, and parental authority and discipline."[13] Whether economic reverses come suddenly or are a part of the family's regular emotional landscape, ongoing economic anxiety often leads to a crisis in a family.

> We'd gotten along pretty well most of our lives. My degree was in chemical engineering, and I had been one of the "hot shots" and fast risers in the small company that hired me right after college. We developed some pretty exciting products in those early years. But as the company grew and got some visibility, it was taken over by a large pharmaceutical firm. Most of us old-timers were out. They figured we just didn't fit into the new corporate culture, I guess. I could barely bring myself to tell June. She had a good job, but the house we were buying, the two kids in college and one a senior in high school, all meant that we had to have both of our salaries just to make ends meet. There was so much at stake. I felt pretty worthless, as if I was letting the whole family down. I didn't know what it was going to mean.   (Victor)

Family therapist Frank S. Pittman III contends that "sudden and unexpected changes in the family's economic status can be extraordinarily disruptive."[14] Marriages are in danger of failing when they are invaded by either wealth or poverty. The unattractive aspects of poverty are too well-known to belabor. However, wealth is bad for marriages too. Victor was worried because he and his wife previously had been able to afford everything they wanted, thus they have little experience in compromising. Because of new economic constraints, they may have difficulty negotiating their marital expectations as well.

Sudden economic change disrupts families in ways that call for promising again. But chronic economic stress on couples in the early years of marriage may impede the process of forming an enduring bond in the first place. Both spouses may have to work long hours just to survive financially or to live in a manner to which they have become accustomed. Just getting by may require investments of time and energy that undermine the couple's investments in each other and in the marriage. At other times, the growing needs and expectations of a young couple may exceed their financial grasp. It is sometimes difficult to know what must change first: the desire to have more than we need *or* an economic system that promotes spending beyond one's means in order to fuel a market that depends on excessive spenders as well as responsible workers.

> Shortly after Miguel and I were married, we bought a small house in the suburbs. We knew it would be difficult to meet the payments, but we thought the sacrifice would be worth it for the equity. Both of us had a long commute to work. We each had one day a week we could call our own but it was not always the same day. The rest of the week, our schedules were such that we barely shared a bed. When our second child was born, we had to move farther out into the suburbs in order to have enough space. The commute became even longer. We had different work schedules in order to care for the children ourselves. The children were cared for and we were financially solvent, but Miguel and I were increasingly becoming strangers to each other. If the children were sick too many days in a month, it was a financial disaster. More than that, I began to resent all the accommodations I was making so that we could have a house that neither of us had time or energy to enjoy either alone or together. (Cheryl)

Cheryl and Miguel's story is a common one. It is, of course, not just a crisis imposed from outside. Their expectations of living "the good life" added to their stress. What looked like a good investment in a home became an emotional and family liability. They intended to be responsible workers, to live well, and to be good parents; this stretched their marital bond to its limits. Their alienation as a couple was a consequence of attempting to do too many things at once. They may decide that spending less will enable them to have more time with their children and each other, but that will be a difficult decision.

Coping with financial reversal requires a strength of partnership in the marriage that avoids either blaming or despair. Responding to the fears and uncertainties of sudden unemployment calls on families to assess their circumstances, conserve resources, and make concrete plans for the immediate and long-term future. When it threatens the family's continuity or health, it may call for a renewal of the marital promise in ways that account for the new, terrifying circumstances of today. Families faced with the chronic drain of unemployment and the resulting stress that threaten the welfare of the marriage may find themselves promising again and again as the vagaries and uncertainties of life take their toll.

The economic instability that many people experience as an ongoing reality in marriage requires a willingness to let go of earlier dreams of what family living would be like. Many couples need to learn how to live with less than they once had and certainly less than they hoped for. In the final chapter of this book, we will consider the necessity of determining the underlying values that govern how families function. Because some economic stress in families is a result of an unwillingness to change dreams, promising again may need to include expecting less. To accomplish that, we need to let go of some treasured dreams. We also need to trust that each partner is doing what he or she can to sustain the family through hard times. Living with economic uncertainty stretches the personal energies of each family member; it also challenges a family's trust in the providence of God.

Psychological and Spiritual Change

Changes occur in persons as well as in families. Illness and death are clear examples, but sometimes the changes are less visible because they occur within. Growth may come through counseling or psychotherapy, from a religious awakening, or because one has responded to a political cause or concern in ways that stimulate new life. Couples also drift apart simply through emotional neglect of each other. When the changes that occur within a partner are significant and enduring, they may upset the delicate balance of the relationship and call for promising again.

Religious or Political Conversion

Religious or political conversions, because they call for such radical commitment of the self, can threaten marriages that otherwise could be gratifying and fulfilling to a couple. The unconverted partner may feel abandoned, marginalized, and unloved. For many couples, the dynamics are similar to an affair except that the "mistress" is usually a visible and socially worthy cause instead of a secret "other."

> When we married, I thought we had quite similar religious hopes and values, although we didn't really talk about it very much. It wasn't that much of an issue. My family wasn't very religious, but we went to church, and we talked about ethical and social issues. Jack's family didn't seem all that religious either, from what I knew of them. So I was shocked when Jack came home from a church service one day and started talking with great energy about his religious "reawakening." He was as charged up as I'd ever seen him about anything, even more than he ever seemed to feel about me or our marriage. That was three years ago. Since then, he's been at the church every Sunday, nearly all day, and there again at least two evenings a week. And when he's home, he's often on the phone with somebody at the church or someone in his prayer group. It seems that all he ever wants to talk to me about is his faith. I love him still, and know we've had a good marriage. But this feels like having a mistress brought into the house before my very eyes. (Valerie)

Valerie's sense of having a mistress in the house is a common experience for partners when their spouse undergoes a sudden or radical conversion to a social or political cause or experiences a religious transformation. Suddenly someone or something else seems more important, maybe even more important than the marriage itself. Much of the emotional energy that was invested in the marriage is taken away and poured into something outside the marriage.

Religious and political conversions can bring about good and desired change. They often are important awakenings and commitments to God and to the world that call people beyond themselves, helping them invest in the broader universe. People do become "new creations" in ways that make them more life-embracing, authentic, and energized persons. But when the transformation of one partner threatens the marriage because it seriously destabilizes the balance in the relationship, couples will be faced with another crisis, demanding that they review their marital commitments and renew them within the context of the new circumstances.

Empathy once again becomes a key to promising again. Both the converted and the nonconverted partner must make every attempt to understand what the other's experiences now are and mean. Judgments need to be suspended by both spouses so that true understanding can occur. Attempts by either partner to convert or deprogram the other will only serve to distance and alienate the spouse. Time also deepens the couple's perspectives about what the new investments mean both to the partner and to the marriage. The willingness to suspend judgment for the sake of understanding requires trust. We are reminded again of the centrality of trust for promising again.

As understanding develops, the marriage needs to be reconfigured in order to acknowledge the new commitments. Where partners can authentically join together in causes important to each other, there is an increased opportunity for marital growth and understanding. If the partner's new cause is too distasteful or calls for activities the partner cannot embrace, the couple may choose to partition this cause from the rest of the marriage, at least until further understanding can develop. In either case, the vitality of the marriage depends on the couple's ability to acknowledge the validity of each other's value systems and commitments, tolerate differences, and to keep open the door of dialogue for matters of critical importance to both.

When conversion (religious or political) becomes a continuing part of the marriage, the couple needs to find ways to reclaim and reestablish priorities. Time at church, at committee meetings, or in community agencies may become important expressions of the spouse's new commitment. Changes in distribution of money will need careful thinking through, no matter how worthy the cause. These new priorities will be more easily integrated into the marriage if both partners make clear and unreserved commitments to each other. When trust is present, promising again is possible even when religious or political conversions threaten to take the couple down separate paths.

Drifting Apart without Malice

The threats to marriage and family that we have discussed so far have included those that happen *to* a family. Deaths and illnesses and lay-offs generally fall outside the spectrum of ordinary family life-cycle development. We turn now to a final threat to marital stability that is less visible and spectacular, less external, yet no less a threat that will call for promising again. We said earlier that the marital bond is formed and sustained by thousands of intended and unintended decisions and commitments. Lack of attention to the relationship is probably the most common reason that marriages do not endure.

> When Carleton retired early from the military, his friends expected him to have difficulty adjusting to life without structure. So did I. During the five years we had been married, we had developed some expensive ways of living. We ate out often and went to the Caribbean whenever we could get a cheap flight. It was a second marriage for both of us, and we were determined to make it work. Carleton retired early partly so I could fulfill a lifelong dream and become a lawyer. Carleton was delighted to have time to work with wood again. We no longer went to the Caribbean. As time went on, a great chasm came to be fixed between my law books and his workbench. We each fulfilled our dreams at the expense of the marriage.
>
> (Suzanne)

Suzanne's story is one shared by many couples at various points in the family life cycle. The demands of raising and supporting families and meeting our own individual needs and goals are genuine and understandable distractions from the work of building and maintaining marriages. Husbands and wives are often pulled in different directions that often become the focus of their attention. The result is distance and disengagement that neither partner intends. Often this is such a gradual process that the chasm created between the partners becomes too wide and fixed before it is recognized or can be amended.

The discovery of the chasm may be precipitated by life-cycle changes such as launching children or retirement, dramatized by an affair, or pointed out by a spouse in despair. Awareness of this distance is often avoided because (1) it has become an integral dimension of the family and (2) calling attention to it upsets the delicate balance that the family has achieved. Even when couples are aware of the distance that has evolved between the partners in a marriage, understanding the causes of the gulf between partners is difficult, particularly if the problem is long-standing. A painstaking inventory is necessary if the couple is to understand the configuration of missed opportunities that have contributed to creating the distance. We will address in the next chapter several approaches that couples in marital trouble may take to bridge the gap.

Compromise and trust are primary aspects of promising again when one partner has undergone dramatic personal or spiritual conversion. For a time, interests that once seemed compatible are in conflict, and the change takes some getting used to. Unlike the first three categories of change discussed in this chapter, emotional and spiritual changes imply the presence of human volition; it appears that partners could have chosen differently. If they are to promise again, each spouse must trust that the other *intends* a new future. Making such a promise in the face of the history of a marriage and the uncertainties of the future is both a necessary and a risky process.

The purpose of this book is to examine ways in which an expected or unexpected crisis may become an occasion for promising again. While a crisis may become a negative experience of loss and stress, it is a turning point or opportunity to choose a direction for life. In each of the crises that we have discussed, we have noted the need for couples to acknowledge their own experiences, share those with each other, and renegotiate their lives together in ways that incorporate the new circumstances they face. Empathic understanding of each other's experiences is vital to this process. Investing again in the re-forming marriage also is essential. When both of those are present, *creative fidelity* is possible. When they are not present, the marriage will flounder.

4
WHEN MARRIAGE FLOUNDERS

THE INITIAL promises in marriage are made without knowing fully what they will mean or what they will cost. We learn the meaning of those promises as we live them out. As each partner grows, and as the relationship changes, we discover new challenges and possibilities of being married. Because change is the norm for family living, staying married is more than keeping a promise. In order to maintain *creative fidelity* in marriage, we need to promise again and again in ways that honor our separate gifts and promote being together. *The meaning of being married evolves as the promises change.*

Sometimes, however, the meaning turns to disappointment and disillusionment. The reality of the marriage as it is lived falls far short of the promise. What we discover about the person we married, or about marriage itself, is not what we expected. Or we may change our expectations of marriage, with or without telling our spouse. One or both of the marital partners may struggle to make sense of what happened to their life together in light of what they hoped for. "For better or worse" may become "what was I thinking of?" At the end of the struggle, one or both partners in the marriage may be unable or unwilling to renew the promise.

What begins as a relationship of great joy and promise can thus become the most frustrating and painful experience in a person's life. We have suggested that promising again is a way of understanding how couples might strengthen their bond when they are confronted by stress or change that throws the relationship off center. This chapter focuses on those moments in marriage when promising again is difficult or perceived to be impossible because the tension is too pervasive or the conflict too intense or the hurt too deep. Moreover, when marriage flounders, it is seldom simply a private matter. The couple's pain is multiplied. Children are wounded. Parents are disappointed, angry, or both. Friends are confused or torn by divided loyalty.

Face to face with couples in conflict, family and friends and caregivers experience first the surprise and pain, and perhaps even the betrayal that the partners have felt. If they listen compassionately and without premature judgment, they are likely to hear one or both of the partners express their rage and remorse and fear. Whenever others are invited to hear the story of a troubled marriage, it is possible to be overwhelmed and powerless in the face of so much pain or to take sides in an unhelpful way. This chapter explores ways of responding as pastoral helpers or friends to couples when their marriage flounders. We hope this chapter will also provide a framework for couples themselves to think about their relationship when it is seriously in need of renewal.

Promises Made Are Not Always Kept

The ability to help people struggle with a disappointing or conflicted marriage or live through a painful divorce begins with an attitude of understanding toward failed promises. Being empathic in such a situation means here, as it always does, suspending judgment. For people in the midst of a painful marriage, the willingness to be empathic with themselves also depends on coming to understand before judgment. If we start with judging the failure in ourselves, in the other person, or even in the relationship as a whole, we limit our understanding of what needs renegotiation or renewal.

Our capacity for empathy is enhanced by recognizing that the cycle of promise-disillusionment-promising again is not new. It is the story of humanity's relationship with God. The biblical story is first about God's promise to the people of Israel, about the promises people have in turn made to God and to each other, their failure to keep those promises, and of the ways the people of God have reclaimed and renewed those promises more than once. Understanding the biblical story of humanity's failure to keep their covenant with God provides a lens through which to view troubled marriages without premature judgment, and then to empathize with those involved.

When the people of Israel determined to renew their covenant with God, they remembered, or were reminded of, the initial covenant. It was this initial promise that called the people to repentance and a renewed covenant both with God and with each other. However, the aim of this recollection was not only to keep the initial promise. The renewal became a new covenant because the circumstances had changed, even though there was continuity with the past. We cannot disregard the past if we intend to hope for a new future. The paradox of continuity and discontinuity finds its expression within the human story and within the biblical story as well.

The renewal of any covenant includes these twin tasks: to recall the initial promise in order to locate the present crisis in the context of the whole story; and to promise again so that the renewed covenant is indeed new. We should not be surprised that promising and promising again are such central experiences in being married and in marrying again. From the perspective of the biblical narrative, it is the human story. We are most free to follow this course of renewal of marriage, as well as in faith, when we begin with the presumption, as part of the human story, that we do not keep all the promises we make.

Promising as a Metaphor
for Responding to Marital Trouble

There are many ways to understand why marriages fail. And each way of interpreting the trouble will propose a method for treating a troubled marriage based on that interpretation. So, for example, if the primary issue is communication, then helping couples renew their bond will focus on modifying distorted communication patterns and enhancing the skill of clear communication. If marriages fail because love dies, then the task is to find ways of restoring love in a disaffected marriage.[1] If the inability to handle conflict and disagreements is what leads to marital trouble, understanding the conflict will lead to developing methods of problem solving in order to maintain respect and connection in the relationship.[2] Similar connections can be made around themes such as power, intimacy, abuse, or addiction, that are linked to marital difficulties.

We propose that the metaphor of promising provides another framework for assessing marital trouble and another way of healing troubled marriages. From this perspective, the major theme is change. The inability of couples and families to adapt to change and to allow room for individuals to change is a fundamental source of marital stress. It is also true that sometimes individuals in a marriage may make more changes than the relationship can bear. Because change is inevitable in family living, marriages remain constant *and* continue to grow if husbands and wives keep promising to one another.

In chapter 1, we developed a framework for understanding promising in marriage that honors both continuity and change. The *primary* promise is the soul of a marriage. It is the promise to love, honor, and cherish another person forever in a covenant of abiding seriousness. From that promise, other dimensions of promising evolve that support and give expression to the *primary* promise. Although we have called them *secondary* promises, they are fundamental to marriages that thrive. There are also *tertiary* promises that keep changing as the circumstances of a marriage change. The daily commitments we make to pick up the laundry at the cleaners or mow the lawn derive from those *tertiary* or time-limited promises. How we respond to the daily promises of marriage will ultimately nurture or damage the *primary* promise.

We have also observed that couples make an initial promise when they begin the process of becoming married. This initial promise may embrace all four dimensions of promising in our model, at least insofar as the couple can know them at the time. For some couples, the initial promise precedes the wedding and is simply the commitment to love, honor, and cherish. For others, the first declaration of the intent to marry includes certain expectations or stipulations regarding the nature of the relationship that resemble what we have referred to as *tertiary* promises.

> When I proposed to Jolene, I was on my way to medical school. For that reason, figuring out the next seven or eight years of our lives became part of our decision to marry. Loving each other would not be enough. We had to envision how the specifics of our life together would work. Jolene's certificate to teach would support us financially. I promised to cook on weekends to give her some time off. After I finished school, however, we expected that I would be able to earn enough to have children, buy a house, and allow Jolene to be home if she wished. We did not anticipate that Jolene would become pregnant in my second year of graduate school.   (Ralph)

The *tertiary* promising that Jolene and Ralph included in their initial promise is increasingly necessary today. The complexity of balancing professional careers, personal growth, the possibility of children, and the work of becoming married make the initial promise for some very complex. They may move from *tertiary* promises to the *primary* promise. For others, however, the wedding vows are still the initial promise. The promise to one another includes God's promised presence. Other promises will follow. Whenever it occurs, however, the initial promise sets the tone for a marriage. The work of becoming married is to relate the initial promise with daily commitments in a way that is faithful to the *primary* promise to love, honor, and cherish one another.

The remainder of this chapter is organized around five questions that couples need to ask themselves or that caregivers may ask in the process of helping couples sort out what happened to the promise. Promising is not a static arrangement that is absolutized or forever fixed once it is made. It is an ongoing, dynamic process that takes into account whatever has changed since the initial promise was made. Remembering the initial promises is therefore a prelude to promising again, so that renewing the promise is an act of *creative fidelity* that goes beyond mere repetition.

Remembering the Initial Promise

Has the Primary Promise Been Made?

We begin with this question because it implies the possibility that some people marry without committing themselves to their partner. That decision often is not a conscious intention. Marriages also are entered out of duty, obligation, or expectation rather than any personal commitment to share one's life with another. "It's a good thing to be married," or "Single persons don't really get ahead in my career," or "Well, I was pregnant so it seemed like the only thing we could do," or "She's just the kind of woman who would make my parents happy" may well be some of the spoken or unspoken circumstances that have led to marriage.

> I was a senior in college and had never really been on my own. I thought I knew myself pretty well, but looking back on it, I figure there was this part of myself I didn't know about—a part that needed someone's help. I'd never really run a household, or even an apartment, and Altoria seemed to know just what to do. She got tired of that pretty quick, so the marriage only lasted eight months. I think I fell in love with her competence and her capacity to do things for me that I didn't realize I could do for myself. (Danville)

Danville could have done just as well with a personal maid or butler. He wanted someone to take care of his needs. In spite of what he said to others at the time, he probably thought he was following the rules of marriage, even though he did not remember making any personal commitment or promise to Altoria. Behind the question Has the *primary* promise been made? is the assumption that making a promise is an intentional act. We may fall in love but we do not fall into marriage. Becoming married requires conscious intention. We also assume that making a promise is personal and relational. No one can do it for us. Promising is not the same as Danville's falling in love with competence. It is relational because we promise to another person rather than to an ideal or an expectation.

What Was the Initial Promise?

The initial promise may have been impulsive and casual or carefully negotiated and formal. For some people, the memories of the initial promise are unambiguous and shared. For others, the memories are distant and clouded. When couples remember the initial promise to each other, they may find an unsettling contrast between the beginning of their marriage and their present struggle. The comparison may help couples understand their present crisis. Others may insist that the initial promise itself was a mistake. Recalling the initial promise does not necessarily reveal what went wrong or offer a solution. Nonetheless, it is a helpful prelude to promising again.

This question is difficult for people who have been married awhile or whose memory is vague. It may generate new tension if what one spouse remembers as the initial promise conflicts with the memory of the other. And it may be embarrassing for people like Danville when their motivation for marriage is revealed. For some people, marriage is a rite of passage, a way to leave home or achieve adult status in the family or culture, rather than a commitment to intimacy or a shared life. What some couples discover when trying to recall what the promise was, is that the initial promise, beginning the process of becoming married, never happened. Remembering honestly comes before repentance.

Because what is remembered is often problematic for one or both of the marital pair, it is crucial that empathy abound. As partners tell the histories of their marriages and realize the variety of reasons they had for marrying at all, the hollowness of their earlier commitments may become painfully clear. Being empathic with ourselves and each other will enhance the possibility of persisting in an occasionally painful process of recollection. These moments of painful discovery are critical times for decision-making about the relationship. The hoped-for outcome of this discovery process is that what did not happen then, could occur now.

To Whom Was the Promise Made?

This can be a deceptively simple question that, nonetheless, bears asking. The obvious answer is "to my partner," but the reality is often different. Authentic answers to this question require sensitive listening and careful probing. It is often hard for people to hear the real answers. The following list suggests some possible answers to the question to whom was the promise made.

—Some have made the promise to their first lover or a secretly beloved person other than their spouse.

—Some have promised to an ideal spouse—to someone they imagined their partner would become.

—Some make promises more to their parents or to the image of the person their parents expected them to marry.

—Others make career commitments that require them to marry certain kinds of spouses for the sake of their success.

—Still others "marry the owner's daughter" in order to assure themselves a steady job.

In any of these cases, the promise is not truly made to the partner, but to someone or something else. Again, remembering the initial promise may lead to a renewal or restructuring of the covenant, if it evokes repentance for having promised in a misleading or unintended, yet inauthentic way.

From a religious perspective, there is a genuine sense in which the initial promise was made to God and the community of faith as well as to the marital partner. When this has been a focus in a couple's faith preparation for marriage, this kind of promise can serve as an embracing frame within which to hold each other and the relationship. Even so, couples often need help to understand that they have been faithful to their commitments to God and the faith community even if their promises to one another in marriage have been altered by the stresses of living in this time.

Promising to God and the community of faith becomes an impediment to promising again and the vitality of a marriage if strict adherence to the particularities of the initial promise is demanded without flexibility or adaptation to the inevitable changes that life presents. That is, when the initial promise is valued over the *primary* promise, the result is a rigid view of marriage and of each partner's expectations of the other. Growth and development for both marriage partners and for the marriage itself is stifled. The only alternative is to keep the initial promise. When that is the pattern, it becomes a marriage in which promising again is quite unlikely.

The possibility of promising again increases when hidden roadblocks to intimacy are admitted and cleared away. Admitting that there are secret loyalties to parents or competing commitments to a job or hidden attachments to idealized images of the other in the marriage is never easy. Pastoral helpers and couples themselves need to remember that acknowledging these roadblocks to a marriage will be enhanced by an attitude of understanding without judgment. We are reluctant to let go of these secret loyalties because they often form a safety net in case the marriage fails. They may also be the reason that the promise was not made initially. In order to promise again or for the first time, however, we need to let go of these secret loyalties.

Why Was the Promise Not Made?

There are several avenues for exploring this question. One has to do with an incomplete resolution of developmental issues such as difficulties with trust or intimacy or lack of self-esteem. The failure to achieve the capacity for fidelity and loyalty may also be linked to the development agenda. For persons who have not satisfactorily resolved life-cycle crises of identity and intimacy, the capacity to make a true commitment to another in any intimate relationship is truly hampered. Erik Erikson has observed that human beings learn fidelity—the ability to remain faithful to promises they make—during adolescence. The primary life-cycle task is to develop ego identity, a congruent and consistent sense of self. It is "the accrued confidence that one's ability to maintain inner sameness and continuity . . . is matched by the sameness and continuity of one's meaning for others."[3] In Erikson's schema, the establishment of a clear sense of self is a prerequisite for intimacy, entering into the life of another with integrity.

> Matt was a really attractive guy when we were in college. He
> was charming, bright, enthusiastic, and outgoing. I felt lucky to
> catch him. It wasn't until after we got married that I saw his
> other side. He would work his way to the top at his job very
> quickly. Before long he'd tire of it, grumble, and then look for
> another job. He was thrilled when our son was born a year af-
> ter we married. He would come home early from work, bring-
> ing gifts on the spur of the moment. But I guess he got tired of
> that too. Before long, he was staying away longer and longer,
> and then one night he just didn't come home at all.   (Emily)

There are persons like Matt who seem to be unable to feel whole
or complete or experience themselves in ways they can trust over time.
This inability to feel certainty within oneself will undermine the capacity to make a commitment to another. Fidelity becomes an unimag-
ined ideal. The sources for such difficulty may lie in wounds deeply
hidden in the past. Or they may lie with events or persons more easily
detected, such as disturbed family relationships or early loss in family.
But the result is an emotional and spiritual self not fully formed, a self
that seeks others for completion or for domination rather than for partnership. The result also is an inability to promise, to keep the promises
that are made, or to promise again.

For troubled couples, attention also might be directed to whether
both partners have left home. Some marriages flounder because one or
both partners have been unable to "leave father and mother" in order to
"cleave" to wife or husband. In another book in this series, *Becoming
Married,* the focus is on the importance of gaining enough emotional
separation from the home of one's origin so that one can commit to another for the sake of forming a new family.

> Natalie and I met at work. It was a passionate relationship from
> the start. We were married after a short courtship. As soon as
> we arrived home from the honeymoon, Natalie started calling
> her mother every day. At first I figured it was her way of ad-
> justing to marriage, but after some months, it only got worse.
> When I complained, she got angry and said her mother was
> her best friend. She'd talk to her mother for hours on end—
> much more than we ever talked to each other. There was noth-
> ing left for me to hold onto.   (Les)

The inability to leave home is a fundamental impediment to becoming married. Natalie was not free to marry Les in a full and emo-

tional sense because of the bond with her mother. Sometimes the hidden loyalties keeping us tied to our families of origin do not become evident until after we are married. Remembering the initial promise intensifies an awareness of family claims that have limited commitment. Individuals in marriage may need help to renegotiate the relationships with their families of origin in order to free themselves for fuller commitment to the marriage.

What Was the Nature of the Promise?

There are always hidden expectations of one's spouse or of the marriage in the initial promises we make. These expectations might be conscious and communicated to the partner, conscious but not communicated to the partner, or not conscious and not communicated to the partner. How will household chores be shared? Who will carry responsibility for financial income and management? How will affection be displayed? What will be permitted in relationships outside the marriage? What are husbands and wives like? How do married people get along? How do parents raise their children? When these questions are asked and answered internally by one or both of the marital partners but not shared with the other, hidden expectations are created.

Sometimes these expectations are even hidden from the person who has them. Often, however, expectations in marriage are kept hidden (1) to test the partner's love ("If he really loved me, he would know what I need."), or (2) because we fear rejection of our secret desire ("If she says no, I will be hurt."), or (3) because we are embarassed by our wishes. Family therapist Clifford Sager has identified the consequences of expectations or "contracts" in a marriage.[4] If the marriage meets most of these expectations and needs, a satisfying marriage is likely to result. If these contracts are not fulfilled, there is resulting damage to the marriage and to the partners within the marriage.

We often choose a marriage partner to meet leftover unconscious needs from our homes of origin. These marriages, Harville Hendrix observes in his book *Getting the Love You Want,* include "all the hidden desires and automatic behaviors that are left over from childhood and that inexorably lead couples into conflict."[5] Hendrix believes that *all* people who marry are unconsciously seeking to establish a relationship in which they can work through issues they were never able to complete with their own parents. When these contracts are invisible, or operate outside the couple's awareness, they make the couple more vulnerable to an incomplete marriage or to a relationship characterized by power struggles and conflict.

There are at least three steps in dealing constructively with hidden contracts: first, becoming aware of the contracts, second, articulating the contracts, and third, explicitly negotiating the contracts with our partners. Expectations that we are already aware of but have not articulated must be spelled out. If a partner can respond and meet the expectation, the marriage will move toward health. If the expectations cannot be met, either in this relationship or at all, couples may need help in either reconstructing the marriage or modifying the partners' internal expectations. It is difficult to modify expectations that are out of our awareness. If an atmosphere of understanding without judgment is present, one's marital partner may be the most helpful "detective" in uncovering hidden expectations.[6]

Although the impulse for helpers and couples alike may be to set in motion a process for renegotiating and renewing the marital bond, it is important that we *not assume* either partner's willingness to enter that process. A premature attempt at promising to each other could simply repeat the premature promise to marry in the first place. Pastors or other helpers should patiently explore with both partners what interfered with their promising in the first place so that those barriers can be dealt with before attempting again to promise. Waiting is part of promising. One cannot hurry the transformation of the soul of a marriage.

When Promises Are Made to More than One

Having an affair is a complex circumstance in marriage for which promising again is both very difficult and absolutely essential if the marriage is to endure. It threatens the *secondary* promise of exclusivity. For some people, having an affair reflects an inability to make intimate commitments. For others, it is an expression of their inability or unwillingness to live with limits. Promising is, by definition, limiting. Because the foundational promise includes exclusivity, an affair is inevitably a betrayal of trust. It is a violation of the promise to one's spouse to "forsake all others."

We are using the term *affair* to refer specifically to a secret, deeply affectional relationship with someone outside the marriage, whether it involves sexual intercourse or not. Affairs are characterized not only by their secretiveness but by their static quality. In other words, couples are not necessarily moving toward a more permanent or publicly acknowledged relationship by choosing to leave their present commitment to begin a new one. Part of what is problematic in these relationships is a desire to keep both relationships intact: to continue the marriage and the extramarital relationship as well. It is generally characterized by its dishonesty.

The vow of exclusive commitment is violated when a marital partner promises to more than one person. And the promises made to a lover are almost always incomplete. We have all heard stories of men and women who promise to leave a spouse for a lover, but months and years pass without change. Those hollow promises mask an unwillingness or inability to make enduring commitments to anyone.

Promising again after a spouse has had an affair requires a capacity to forgive that goes far beyond what either partner has experienced before. The pain and hurt and anger generated by an affair can be overwhelming. For some couples, the discovery that a spouse has had an affair almost automatically ends the marriage. *For couples to get past hurt and blame, two things are required simultaneously: a confession and admission of betrayal and an exploration of circumstances that contributed to either brokenness in the relationship or a lingering dissatisfaction in the marriage.* Couples who survive the initial betrayal and shame of such experiences can frequently find new life and hope in the careful rebuilding of their relationships. The journey back to promising again requires hard work, determination, and an abundance of good will.

The process of renewing a covenant shattered by infidelity is made difficult by two opposite outcomes. If the betrayal is not taken seriously enough, the memories and wounds of the affair will likely remain, though often hidden from view. If the affair continues to define the relationship, however, and a heavy residue of blame and shame remain, one partner will continue to live with moral inferiority and the powerlessness that comes with its discovery. The other partner will carry the burden of moral superiority, a lifelong self-image as the wronged one who must forever be pampered at all costs. What is called for is a process that acknowledges both the confession and the forgiveness, both the reality of sin, and the response of grace.

Promising Again When a Marriage Is Troubled

The consideration of what is necessary to heal a marriage that has been devastated by an affair exemplifies what is needed whenever couples must promise again in the midst of a troubled marriage. What follows are a number of methods or strategies that pastoral helpers or couples might use to enhance the possibility of successful promising again.

Remembering the Initial Promise

An honest rehearsal of the beginning of any marriage is often the occasion for pain and confusion. It is particularly a risky thing to remember the initial promises. Partners may discover that the marriage began with conflicting promises. The absence of an initial promise is a painful truth that leaves some couples angry or in despair. Some find an emptiness in relation to what they thought they had. Others feel angry at being betrayed or deceived (albeit unintentionally). When the discovery occurs in an empathic context, it may lead to repentance as a prelude to promising for the first time.

Renegotiating Unmet Expectations

Couples who are able, with or without help, to ferret out hidden agendas and confront them honestly are on the road to promising again. Once uncovered, expectations and hidden contracts can be renegotiated, and more realistic agreements can be made more intentionally.

Making the Unconscious Conscious

Often the promise has been made in covert ways; an *unconscious marriage* was formed by partners who were not even aware of what they were seeking from each other. When couples have made these less-than-obvious commitments, the task is to renegotiate the relationship to meet those needs in more realistic and fulfilling ways.

Recognizing Lost Opportunities

Missed chances to promise again may be more damaging than no chances at all. Such oversights may lead to an accumulation of hidden resentments or a smoldering sense of ineffectiveness and bitterness. We need to celebrate the changes in a family when they occur. When a wife stops drinking, or when a husband gives up overtime to be home more and no one notices, couples have not recognized chances to renew the marriage covenant. One partner may have made a private decision to change and not warned others who will be affected by the change. There is a magical expectation that others will respond positively to the change they say they've been wanting so long, even without knowing that it's really coming. Declaring one's intention to change prepares the family and enlists their help.

Imagining a Renewed Covenant

Couples who are able to uncover the hidden and disclose the unknown may achieve a fresh comprehension of the promises they first made to each other. However, they still may need help to imagine ways in which that promise can be remade. For these couples, the difficulty has been in their inability to imagine ways that a renewed promise may become vital and fulfilling given the way things have turned out. They have lost any sense of alternatives, and see no options from which to choose. Imagining possible alternatives for change with couples is often a very helpful strategy.

Getting the Help We Need to Promise Again

It is a fearful thing when a marriage starts to spiral out of control. Some couples are able to find healing relationships that help them pull together those pieces of self that threaten to fly apart. Others run from relationship to relationship, or move into isolation in despair, rather than confront the emptiness within. It is a terrifying thing to acknowledge the gaps in self. Most of us cannot do it alone. Even if we have the courage to confront that reality, in order to grow we need a trusted counselor, steady friends, and a community of faith to walk with us toward the light of promising again.

Celebrating the New Promise

Promising again calls for celebration. In fact, without acknowledgment and enactment of the new promise, the promise itself fails to become real. The partner who plans to change must declare the intention to change, so that partners and family members can anticipate and participate in the change. Partners who have asked for change, for a new promise, can enhance the power of the promise by recognizing and appreciating the change when it comes. Where hurts have accumulated to volcanic proportions, such appreciation will be hard to muster. But without the act of promising again, the marriage is likely to explode.

Encouraging couples to promise again in the company of family, friends, and faith communities has at least two aims. It continues to support the public nature of marriage. That purpose is fulfilled when significant anniversary dates are noted in the context of a worshipping congregation. When anniversaries are celebrated more often than every twenty-five years, the responsibility of communities to support marriage is encouraged. The regular practice of promising again also teaches the community about the dynamic nature of promising. When couples promise publicly after a major destabilizing crisis has been endured or when adaptation to major change has created a new constancy, they invite others to celebrate the newness of life. In turn, the religious congregation creates a context that encourages promising again as an ongoing dimension of living in the covenant of marriage.

When Promising Again Does Not Work

Promising to another is the heart of a relationship. It is what keeps marriages vital and enables them to endure. Sometimes, however, promising again is not possible, and the marriage ends. When our promises to another dissolve, our connectedness and trust disappear with them. One of the most difficult tasks for caregivers and friends often occurs when couples they have cared for conclude that their marriage cannot continue.

Whether the dissolution of the marriage is brought about because of abuse (physical or emotional), by the uneven growth of the partners, or by the decision of one partner, marriages do end. Unfortunately, many couples are left on their own to work through the painful process of separating, divorcing, and caring for their children. At least, they often must undergo these transformations without the help of the community of faith, who have seen it as their obligation only to keep people together, and who are not available to help those for whom continuation in the marriage is no longer possible.

> Many of the people at my church were surprised when I told them I was getting divorced. My husband did not go to church. Some of the members even joked about my "phantom husband." He did show up often enough that people recognized him when they saw him. None of my friends knew about the

counselors I talked to or the marriage therapist we saw. People asked me if I'd really tried to make my marriage work. It hurt
that they had no clue about how bad things were, or that they
thought that somehow I had the power to make or break the
marriage. Maybe they didn't notice on purpose. But then, I had
not been very revealing with them either—at least until the
end.   (Maureen)

The end of a marriage is often a secret sadness. Maureen's divorce
was a surprise to her friends but not to her. For the people at church, it
looked as if her marital crises opened up "out of the blue." Sometimes
a troubled marriage "sneaks up" on family and friends. Occasionally
the request for a divorce is a totally unexpected shock, even to the other
partner in the marriage. Cracks can open up in marriages that look to
everyone else like solid ground. Most of the time, however, warning
signs appear when marriages are in trouble.

The end of a marriage is difficult for friends and family. People
find it difficult to maintain warm friendships with both divorcing partners. The anger and hurt that is experienced by divorcing persons and
directed toward their partners may force friends to take sides. Wounded
partners question the loyalty, and even the morality, of friends who
maintain contact with the wounding partner. Church members question
the pastor's contact with one who is known to be causing the divorce.
Members or pastors whose own marriages feel shaky may experience
too intensely the sense that "there, but for the grace of God, go I."
Whatever the reason, persons in the midst of marital breakup often find
themselves alone.

Ritualizing the End of a Marriage

Public declaration and rituals of divorce may bring about a deeper
healing of relationships and a move toward wholeness in ways not otherwise possible. Marking such a profound transition is important for
former partners, who now go their separate ways. It could be important
for members of their significant communities to participate in or even
hear of the ritual event. But the greatest benefit of the ritual might fall
to the children involved, for whom divorce is at best a wrenching and
confusing time.

Tom Driver outlines several functions that ritual has in the lives of
human beings. He notes that some realities, in fact, do not become real
until they are enacted—until ritual brings them into being.[7] If such is

true for the reality of divorce, we could argue that without some ritual acknowledgment of the separate lives of the two divorcing partners, there is no divorce, at least in the minds of the performers and the public who would participate with them. This is undoubtedly one of the reasons the church has been reluctant to offer rituals of divorce, as though the church would then be participating in the reality of something that it opposes.

On occasion there are divorcing partners who wish to be alone. For some, this is a time for healing and prayer, and for others, it is prompted by a sense of shame or awareness of the community's condemnation. We believe that our approach to such persons is best accomplished by sensitivity to the member's privacy, while communicating our emotional and spiritual availability. On other occasions, more active offers of time together are called for.

The sad truth is that for some couples, promising again will not occur. Some couples keep the initial promise unchanged for the sake of the children. These couples survive in hollow shells of marriages, occasionally managing to maintain appearances of family tranquility. For others, even the best help may not be enough. With some marriages ending in these painful circumstances, the church's presence becomes crucial, though difficult. Yet the gospel of hope is intended for all who would hear. And for these, promising again may take still another shape—promising to another in marriage.

5

WHEN MARRYING AGAIN

PROMISING IS a fundamental human activity. Probably no
single promise makes that declaration so pointedly as does
the wedding ceremony. We promise for the future in marriage. Couples build their hopes and dreams around visions of spending the rest of their life together, images of growing old together, and
fantasies of living "happily ever after." No one stands at the altar during a wedding expecting the marriage to end.

> I married for the second time several years ago. One day my
> husband's daughter was talking about her mother's upcoming
> wedding. She was excited and curious, wondering about all
> the planning and extravagant detail that was going into the
> wedding. I tried to explain it to her. "Well, you only get married
> once in life." I was stunned when I realized what I had said.
>
> (Elizabeth)

Elizabeth's forgetfulness is understandable. We expect to keep a
promise when we make it. There are, however, an increasing number
of people for whom marriage is a contractual agreement for a limited
period of time that anticipates the distribution of property in the event
of a divorce. In an age of nonbinding commitments and maximum individual options, it is not surprising that people promise to one another
for "as long as it is convenient" or "as long as it is good for us." Not
everybody expects permanence in marriage.

The religious tradition of permanence in marriage and the romantic ideal of love for a lifetime both have been severely challenged by
a variety of modern factors. As noted earlier, promising now must
last longer than ever before. Longer life expectancy, greater financial

freedom for women, and the increased acceptance of divorce all have contributed to fewer marriages surviving until the physical death of one of the partners. Greater mobility of our society and the breakdown of continuing, close relationships with extended family also have influenced this change. There are thus more options available to couples in conflict.

Up to this point in this book, *promising again* has been understood as a renewal of commitment necessary to keep any relationship alive and growing, an action that needs to be taken whenever there is a significant change in a relationship. Promising again takes place in the *ordinary* transitions of life — when children enter a family and again when they leave a family. Promising again also takes place in the *extraordinary* transitions of life — when disaster strikes, when a geographical move occurs or when a spouse goes back to school or loses a job. We promise again when an alcoholic spouse recovers from disease or when a spouse or a spouse's parent becomes dependent due to chronic illness.

For an increasing number, the persons to whom we promise again wear new faces. *Promising again can mean marrying again.* Because people live longer, the possibility of a second marriage occurring is greater. Increasingly, this will mean that marriages of those in mature years will often be second marriages. Moreover, the frequency of divorce does not appear to have diminished the likelihood that people will marry again. Even for those who least anticipate it, marrying again has become thinkable. Second and even third marriages have increasingly become a regular landmark of the cultural landscape.

Although the primary aim of this book is to develop the regular practice of promising again for the sake of strengthening family living, we also use the same metaphor to refer to people who marry again after divorce or the death of a spouse. We are aware that there are differing theological beliefs and consequent practices regarding divorce and remarriage particularly after divorce. Within some religious traditions, persons do not have the option either to divorce or remarry after divorce, and sometimes must leave their faith community in order to leave their marriage. By denying the possibility of remarriage, some Christian traditions have increased the shame of divorce and thereby unwittingly privatized marriage further by insisting that second marriages do not belong in the church. Each religious tradition struggles to maintain integrity with their understanding of faithful Christian living while at the same time ministering to people whose marriages are floundering. We need to increase our public understanding of marriage in order to provide a context for the tasks of promising again. Divorcing persons and those who remarry need the support of communities of faith in order to undergird their transition to a new life.

In this chapter, we explore second marriages after a spouse's death or after divorce, what they have in common and how they are different. Our aim is to examine the use of the metaphor of *promising again* in relation to second marriages. In what ways does promising again deepen our understanding of the issues of marrying again? How is it similar and how is it different to make a new commitment when the initial promise fails? And what are the differences between marrying again after divorce and after a spouse's death?

Starting Again

Standing at the altar for a second time, this time with someone else, seems like starting over again with a new chance at life and love. It is a moment fraught with apprehension and filled with hope. We imagine a clean slate to begin writing on, a fresh page for drawing new pictures. With this new partner, there are fewer wrongs to forgive or early promises to renegotiate. Marrying again, however, is not the same as the initial promise in three specific ways: first, there is a deeper experience of loss; second, one must incorporate the reality of the previous spouses, friends, and family members; and third, partners in a second marriage after divorce approach this promise as sadder but wiser persons because they know firsthand that marital failure is possible.[1]

A Second Marriage Is Born in Grief

Promising again is invariably an *experience of loss,* just as surely as it is a declaration of hope in the future. When people promise again in the same marriage partnership, there may be a *shared history* that must be grieved as the couple moves to the next stage of life together. There are significant changes that occur in individuals within the relationship, as well as the marital bond itself, because of professional development, religious conversion, personal transformation, or other forms of growth that may need to be mourned as well as celebrated. Even those who promise again in the same marriage will experience some grief.

When we promise again to another person, the grief experience is more pervasive. We must grieve former relationships in order to be free to embrace the new one. In becoming married again, we may need to leave behind central relationships that have defined our life and our self. The following story illustrates one way for couples marrying again to honor people who have been significant in their past. It is a ritual of incorporation as well as a ritual of grieving.

> My new husband's first wife had died of cancer five years be-
> fore we married. It had been a good marriage. She was at the
> center of his life and they had been partners in raising their
> three children. They also had an extraordinary network of
> friends, some of whom had become my friends as well. We
> wanted to recognize in our wedding ceremony all those peo-
> ple who had shaped our lives in significant ways but were not
> with us on our wedding day because of death, time, or dis-
> tance. Instead of the traditional unity candle, we had concen-
> tric circles of light representing those people. During the ser-
> vice, we named each of them out loud. I was very glad I had
> not worn eye make-up. There wasn't a dry eye in the place, in-
> cluding mine.   (Martha)

Much is new for those who marry again. The discontinuities far exceed the continuities. The grief is more public than for those who renew their wedding vows, because the divorce or death is common knowledge. For the couple, however, the grief still is personal. There are *separate histories* rather than shared ones that individuals must release.[2] There are also *separate stories* that must be grieved. Persons marrying for the second time bring longer histories and more painful losses to the wedding ceremony. Marrying again means letting go. Therein lies grief.

Incorporating the Past

When we marry again, we modify the self as it has come to be. Persons who were significant to us, even in painful or destructive ways, are nonetheless still part of us. We are aware, in retrospect, of past relationships that have shaped us. The way a former husband used to scrub the kitchen floor every night seemed obsessive to his wife at the time, but even after the divorce she is tidier than she used to be. Or it may be his handiness with tools that she thought was his way of avoiding her by spending time in his workshop, until he dies and she misses the smell of sawdust. Former spouses have informed our enduring impressions of what women and men are like, or what wives or husbands or mothers or fathers ought to be.

When there are children involved, separation is not absolute. The presence of former spouses is most dramatic in second marriages when children are present. The continuing care for children is an unbreakable bond between former spouses, and it also provides a frequent arena for conflict. Children inevitably bring the presence of a divorced parent into the home of a second marriage. Following the death of a parent, and the eventual remarriage of the surviving spouse, children (even adult children) sometimes resent the presence of the new spouse. They may insist on keeping alive the memory of the deceased parent in order to distance the surviving parent's new spouse.

Even in cases where there are no children to carry the presence of the former spouse, that former spouse lives on in significant ways. New relationships get into trouble whenever spouses refuse to acknowledge the presence of former partners. Marrying again nearly always brings with it a large cast of characters to be united in the new household. Children and parents, friends and co-workers, in-laws and step-children create a complex, emotionally charged network in which a second marriage occurs. Some come willingly, even eagerly. Others come only reluctantly, if at all. Some enter at once, and others take their time before joining the new family. Some may be unable or unwilling to join at all. Finding ways to hold places for those who find it hard to join is an important task for those who marry again.

Wiser the Second Time

Persons marrying for a second time are often more aware of the complexities of *promising again*. We have described promising at the time of marriage as a promise for the future before we can possibly know all that it means. This is equally true for those who are marrying again. And yet, partners entering second marriages often have some awareness of what the future may hold. They have knowledge of what the new spouse is like as a parent or how he or she handles stress. The stories from a first marriage are some indication of the future to which two promise in a new bond. Even so, there will be surprises. Nothing can be taken for granted. For that reason, promising again in a second marriage also deepens the joy and appreciation for new love.

Marrying after Death Is Different from Marrying after Divorce

Second marriages share a common sense of starting again. They share the complexity of bringing together friends and relatives who might have no other reason to be together. And they share the experience of the presence of former spouses and former relationships. Beyond those similarities, however, there are differences that make remarriage after divorce quite different from remarriage after the death of a spouse.

What Did I Do to Make This Happen?

One of the factors that most dramatically separates the two experiences is the sense of *responsibility or agency.* Following divorce, there is generally a greater sense that one or both persons *caused* or *chose* the end of the former relationship. Most of our theological, cultural, and personal ideas support the notion of personal responsibility in matters of divorce. We are more likely to feel responsible, or to hold our spouse responsible for divorce than we do in the case of our spouse's death.

We are familiar with those who feel remorse or guilt about their treatment of a partner who has died. If those angry feelings and thoughts are not acknowledged, survivors may feel an inappropriate sense of responsibility for the spouse's death. This kind of *magical thinking,* that is, the belief that one's thoughts or words have caused someone's death, usually goes away with time and understanding, except where some realistic doubt about a role in the other's death may continue.

The matter is more complex, however, following a divorce. There is a greater likelihood that *feelings of guilt are present* in matters of divorce. While some divorcing persons truly understand themselves to have been victims in their marriages, others feel responsible for the breakup of the marriage. Whether one was the partner who initiated the separation or the one who was left, both know at some level that their behavior or attitudes or self *caused* the breakup of the marriage. For some, feelings of abandonment predominate; for others, shame is primary. In either case, people marry following divorce *with a greater awareness of the power to choose.* "I choose this marriage as I chose to leave the previous one." Or, paradoxically, "What if I make the wrong choice again?" Either way, the sense of agency or responsibility is a central issue.

Why Must I Keep Running into Him or Her?

The deceased partner of a new spouse continues to be present through family, children, friends, and even the belongings that remain in the house. But reencountering the ex-spouse can become a problem in promising again after divorce. Unresolved feelings of guilt, loyalty, or revenge toward a former spouse make those encounters traumatic and can interfere with new relationships. This is painfully true when there were children from the previous marriage. But even when children are not the issue, there are friends, colleagues, and extended family, as well as business matters and old habits that provide the setting or occasion for encounters, expected or unexpected.

These encounters can be traumatic when they occur at the time of a significant family event, such as a high school or college graduation, the wedding of a child, or a music recital. Often these events evoke memories of dreams and hopes once held, as well as re-evoking the pain of the divorce.

Why Don't They Approve?

Marrying again disrupts systems that may have just started to balance themselves after death or divorce. When that is so, family or friends may subtly undermine the new relationship, trying to prevent more changes. This is usually more common following a divorce than after a death. We are still religiously and culturally more open to new partnerships following death than following divorce. When marriage is held as a lifelong commitment, and when divorce is perceived as moral failure, there is greater likelihood that community support for marrying again will be less available. Even when persons are no longer active participants in those traditions, underlying feelings of guilt and shame sometimes interfere with their capacity to make new commitments.

> My wife developed breast cancer when our children were eight and ten years old. Her final struggle with her illness lasted a year-and-a-half, but she had had two surgeries in the four years prior to that. We had hospice care at home, and so we spent a lot of time with Jennifer right up 'till the end. For the last

nine months of her illness, she was pretty incoherent, partly due to the illness, but mostly due to the medications she was on. She died a quiet death at home.

During her illness, several friends at work were quite supportive. Nancy was one of them. She worked in human resources at my company. She knew of Jennifer's illness because of the insurance. She was quite helpful in working through some of the emotional issues as well as the paperwork. We talked often at work, but nothing romantic developed. During the last few months of Jennifer's illness, I realized how much I was enjoying the conversations with Nancy. Six months after losing Jennifer, Nancy and I decided to marry. The kids took it pretty hard. I think they didn't understand what Nancy meant to me, and how much I needed to have adult company for the rest of my life. I had grieved for Jennifer for two years before her death.   (Daniel)

Daniel's dilemma is not unusual. Nor is it simple. Although we may be religiously or culturally more open to remarriage after the death of a spouse, the emotional dynamics are often the same. Children struggle with a parent's remarriage, especially when they think it is too soon. Mixed in with the positive anticipation of a new adult in the family are feelings of fear and anger that are part of lingering grief. The children also are loyal to the memory of the deceased parent. No one had better dare take father or mother's place in this house! For children of divorce, a parent's marrying again undermines the hope that their parents will get back together. Unspoken fantasies are dashed. When a parent has died, children face the complications and confusions of grief that may come with a *replacement* person in the home.

What is particularly true for children may be present also for other family members and friends. There is an emotional process in either death or divorce that requires time. We need to let go of former persons and relationships so we can less ambivalently enter into new ones. Daniel may have let Jennifer go and started the grieving process even before she died, but the children had not. His decision to marry again did not take fully into account their needs. Timing is one of the most critical factors in forming a new family after death or divorce. Children are more likely to accept new families when there has been sufficient time to grieve former relationships. Above all, talking with children about their fears, hopes, and ideas about new families is essential for those with children who choose to marry again.

It Is Different for Those Who Leave

We began by considering how promising again is different for those who marry for a second time. We also observed that there are some differences between marrying again after a spouse's death and after divorce. There are also differences between chosing to leave a marriage and being left that affect promising again. While there are marriages in which both parties simultaneously conclude that the marriage is no longer viable, it is more common that one partner grows more dissatisfied than the other. That individual is likely to become the "leaver," whereas the other is the one who is "left."

Leavers tend to deal primarily with feelings of *guilt,* that sense of having caused the breakup or having taken the painful action to end the marriage. The partner who wanted to continue the marriage, or who came to a later realization of the need to end the marriage, is more likely to experience *powerlessness* and *hurt.* The one who leaves may feel guilt but also feels in charge of his or her own life. The divorce happens to the one who is left. People left in a divorce feel robbed or betrayed, with little sense of capacity to influence the outcome.

These differing experiences inevitably affect the way in which the persons approach new relationships. The *leaver* may feel more sense of agency in choosing a new relationship than the former partner. The *one who has been left* may feel a sense of hopelessness in being able to establish or maintain a new relationship. Or she or he may also feel a sense of desperation or panic when new relationships begin. Both extremes are as likely to be illusory as they are to be factual. We are limited human creatures. Therefore, none of us is fully capable of guaranteeing any promises, nor are any of us free of responsibility for promising again.

The *left* may feel profound anxiety about her or his ability to hold another to a promise—another aspect of the same sense of agency that may lead the former partner to take too much credit for maintaining the new relationship. These individuals may suffer substantial fear about their *lovableness* and yet desperately need to be loved. Just as the *leaver* may develop an exaggerated sense of control over life, the *left* may underestimate his or her role in initiating and nurturing relationships.

Leavers and the ones who have been left have different pastoral needs during or following divorce. They are likely to approach the process of making a new promise with different understandings about the agency or responsibility of a person. Both will need to explore their own roles in the marital breakup in order to achieve a more balanced perspective on the previous relationship. Both those who leave and those who are left ultimately need the same assurance of God's faithfulness. The healing process around divorce begins with the recognition by both partners that the leaver was also left, and the *left* was also a leaver. Reconciliation is possible after divorce when responsibility is shared, when each person can admit that they are more *like* the one from whom they are divorced than they are *different* from him or her.

Characteristics of Promising Again
Unique to Marrying Again

The characteristics of promising again developed in previous chapters need to be modified if the metaphor is to be used to describe the complex matters of second marriages. The following list of markers begins to identify what we must be alert to in second marriages so that promising again in that context will endure.

1. *Former relationships have been grieved.* Significant involvements with former spouses must be worked through and left behind. Although some continuing emotional investment in the earlier relationship is acknowledged, there is no undue obsession with that person or with the previous relationship. Because grieving is a painful process, it is one that persons frequently avoid. It is also a time-consuming process, providing divorcing persons ample opportunity to reflect on their own roles in the demise of their marriage. While there are often more available structures of support and opportunities for grieving in the event of the death of a spouse, the process of grieving after a divorce is equally as important.

> When I walked past the houses we had lived in, I would become sick and dizzy, mourning a marriage, mourning myself, mourning a boy I loved once. I never thought of myself as divorced, but widowed. Widowhood leaves one more freedom to be sad. I can't go to church much anymore. I look around at the nice Irish couples at St. Joseph's and I wish my husband were beside me and that we were going home to roast pork with onion gravy. I suspect the grieving will never end.
>
> (Claudia)

Claudia's story is an important reminder of the grief of divorce. Even when divorce is mostly relief that an unhappy or violent marriage has ended, there will at least be loss of a dream. We can help divorcing people best by allowing them to grieve. When they can mourn the loss of a dream, it is easier to dream again.

2. *Newly formed couples develop an openness to the reality of the former relationships.* It is a delicate but necessary task that divorcing persons establish appropriate boundaries between themselves and the former spouse. Defensiveness about the decision to divorce or unrelieved hostility toward a former spouse often leads to thick walls of separation and make it difficult for divorced persons to acknowledge the good as well as the bad in past marriages or relationships. Misspoken names at dinner or in the middle of making love, expectations of a new partner that were more appropriate to the former relationship, or accusations of being just like the former spouse suggest to a new partner that the boundaries are not firm enough. Two things are true. The reality of the new promise is embraced more readily when we are free to remember the previous relationship. We remember the past more easily when the present has been transformed by an enduring experience of love. Children also need clear separation from the past so they are free to remember it.

3. *A new marital relationship has a developmental cycle of its own.* As a new marital bond is formed, increasingly there will be less comparing of the present relationships to former relationships or persons, and more building on the new memories that are being formed in the new relationship. As experience and loss are faced and survived, as a new story is being written, the new relationship forms an identity of its own. In fact, the process of becoming married begins again in this new marriage.

4. *Increasingly, a new community is being formed around the new couple.* They are developing a set of friends who belong to this couple, as well as to each partner. New friends are discovered, and some former friends are able to make the transition to the new relationship. This is particularly important in relation to family members. Children, parents, siblings, and sometimes even former in-laws form new alliances. Functional arrangements are developed with ex-spouses and former in-laws; ways of resolving the inevitable problems of living are discovered and developed over time. In short, a new life-sustaining network grows to nurture the new marriage and build a sense of belonging and family again. One word of caution. This new community of nurturing support can exclude as well as include.

5. *Members of the new family become realistic about the differences between this family and former families.* We need to let go of

expectations that we can make this marriage or family *like* the previous one. Even the strongest and healthiest families cannot be replicated. We also need to let go of expectations that we will *avoid* all the pitfalls of the previous relationship. Persons carry their own histories and personality structures with them into new relationships, and some problems in living are due to the very fact of living in families. We cannot repeat the past or avoid it in forming a new family. There is both continuity *and* discontinuity with previous marriages. The hard work of marrying again is to develop a new narrative with unique memories that will be recalled later by this newly formed family.

6. *Children are free to develop and maintain full relationships with both biological parents.* Children need to continue their emotional bonds with the parents who gave them birth. Those who are kept from doing so are more likely to struggle and to create difficulties in the primary care family.

7. *A body of new rituals is formed.* Ways of celebrating holidays, anniversaries, and birthdays are created to fit and express the new realities. From daily routines around mealtime and bedtime to celebrations of Christmas or vacation time, family members (including children) contribute to new ways of doing things and develop new patterns of family life together. Sometimes these rituals carry over the best from previous families while at the same time confirming new family structures. Other rituals come freshly into being as family members are allowed to become creative in their thinking and planning.[3]

8. *There is allowance for the time that it takes to form a new family.* Family research suggests that it requires at least two years for a second marriage to stabilize, and even longer for families with adolescents.[4] Partners who promise again have made choices to do so. Children have not. Granting children the time and space to find their own ways in this new and unchosen family goes far toward ensuring the success of the new family.

9. *An openness to experimentation and a sense of humor are critical.* We are still in the process of developing models for stepfamilies that will provide roadmaps for those who marry into those relationships. Flexibility and creativity mark the families who are staking out new territory.

10. *Couples who marry again may decide to have children of their own.* Such choices can bring with them a unique bonding that helps to transcend the inevitable sense of *yours* and *mine* in regard to children. When such children are conceived in love and give expression to a

deeper commitment to the new marriage, they can be true marks of promising again in enduring ways.

Barriers to Promising in Second Marriages

The *ghosts of former spouses* frequently haunt second marriages. That is to say, grieving the end of a marriage or the death of a spouse never ends. Previous spouses, children who do not live with the new family, even friends who were part of the former family's network, frequently live on in the newly formed family, long after they are physically absent. Expectations of what wives or husbands or children or friends should be like have been shaped and influenced by the reality of those past relationships. These internalized patterns do not go away simply because the marriage is over.

> We were just starting out on a short weekend vacation with the new family. Vacations had been one of the few aspects of my first marriage that I had enjoyed. I'd almost always looked forward to getting away from home—maybe because home itself had stopped being a pleasant place to be some years earlier. So starting out now with my new family I had this sense of déjà vu for a moment or two. We were just about to turn a corner at a stoplight when I asked my wife to check the map. I called her by my first wife's name. (Nate)

In new relationships, persons must find ways to acknowledge the *continuing presence of the former relationship*. There could have been many reasons Nate used his first wife's name. The important point for a second marriage is for everyone to remember that grieving never ends. Important relationships become a permanent part of our life experience and memory. One way in which married-again couples are able to address this reality positively is to intentionally develop the ability to appreciate what was good about the former relationship and about the former spouse and to speak openly about those memories.

> Maurice and I had each lost a spouse through death. We had also both been very happily married. We knew about being married but we did not know about being married to each other. I really needed time to adjust to the fact that Maurice was very different from my first husband. Our pastor had been very good at insisting that we talk through many things before we got married. For example, we agreed that each of us would be buried with our previous spouse. About a month after we

> were married, Maurice visited the grave of his first wife. It was
> my first visit. When I saw the name Maurice and his birth date
> on *their* gravestone, I began to sob. We decided that we
> needed to discuss again where we would be buried. (Wilma)

It is a lot easier to adjust to a new marriage when everyone is free
to acknowledge ambivalent feelings. The new marital bond between
Maurice and Wilma will be strengthened because they could talk together about whether to be buried with former spouses. Even when a
divorce has been bitter and angry, there are some positive feelings left
about the marriage or the former partner. An unwillingness to recognize those feelings can contribute to a level of unconscious dishonesty
and an inability to develop fuller intimacy in the new relationship.

From their beginnings, families are part of a *network of extended
communities* of extraordinary complexity and breadth. As mentioned
earlier, in new relationships there generally is the involvement of an entire cast of characters from previous relationships, each of whom is in
one way or another either to be brought into the new relationship or left
outside. In a culture that values individuality as highly as ours does, the
privacy of choice in matters related to marriage often undermines the
corporate nature of marriage. Couples who are unable to form new supportive communities, or whose communities offer only anger or conflict, will struggle on their own to build a new marriage. Couples who
develop supportive communities of faith, of family, and of friendship
often build for themselves networks of support for the inevitable difficulties of life.

> My children were about to leave for college when I remarried.
> My new wife brought to our marriage two daughters, ages
> seven and ten, who were warm and receptive to our relation-
> ship, in spite of the understandable confusion and restriction
> that it meant for them. I'd anticipated enjoying their growing up
> and participating in the events of school and friends that I'd so
> enjoyed with my own kids. At times, though, I would feel a sad-
> ness, both out of the loss of those times with my own kids, and
> a heaviness about "You mean I have to go through this all
> again? Didn't I do this once already?"   (David)

In *The Changing Family Life Cycle,* Carter and McGoldrick[3] note
the substantial difficulties faced by couples in second marriages who
are themselves at different phases in the family life cycle.[5] As David
discovered, partners who have launched their children and anticipate

time alone with a new spouse and friends frequently find themselves back into the routines of child care, chauffeuring, and soccer games. Even partners who care for their stepchildren and enjoyed the activities of their own biological children may silently chafe under the reimposed constrictions. Partners who are earlier in their own family life cycles sometimes resent the demands of forming relationships with children they didn't raise and who seem to draw energy away from their own biological children. They face the possible threat of new older children who take over some of the parenting or role model functions the partner coveted for him- or herself, or who model behaviors and attitudes the parent doesn't want influencing his or her own younger children.

Marrying again stands squarely on the shoulders of faith. For those who are survivors of failed marriages, or those who have watched a spouse die, entering again into intimacy with another is risky business. And it is a risk some choose not to take. For many, the pain and the grief of past marriages stand between them and promising again. There is *a loss of faith in promises.* Watching a person or a relationship die kills the wish to join, to belong, to be close, and to care in that most intimate of all ways. For some, it represents a decision not to love again, for fear of losing or failing again. For others, the experience leads to cynicism, a belief that marriage is "not for me" or that "people weren't really meant to live forever in marriages." Still others may keep faith in promising but not marry again for various reasons.

There is a continuum of faith in making the marital promise again, stretching from "total cynicism" on one hand to "cheap grace" on the other. Some couples have married too easily, without acknowledging the pain of earlier losses or the role of one's own behavior in hurting another. Other individuals have been embittered by divorce or death of a spouse to the extent that they have been unwilling to consider deep involvement with another. Their pain has led them to loneliness and isolation; their lack of faith in a God who stands behind our promises has separated them from intimacy. The hope of promising again is in acknowledging both the limitedness of our ability to keep all of our own promises and the faithfulness of the One who promises to us.

Pre-Wedding Preparation for Second Marriages

It is necessary to leave home in order to become married. This biblical and psychological truth is applicable for all marriages. There is no certainty that people who have been married before, left home enough to become married. When the first marriage recapitulates the dynamics of an individual's family of origin, the work of leaving may be unfinished. Sometimes, leaving a first marriage is itself a differentiating act. Leaving a marriage may be the first time a person defines herself or himself apart from the values and pressures of his or her family of origin. While divorce may be a dramatic statement of personal authority, it is too reactive to complete the task of establishing emotional separation from the home of one's origin.

For that reason, one purpose of pre-wedding preparation remains constant: to clarify and enhance the process of leaving home. "The pastoral pre-wedding task is to link the legacies from their families of origin with the values of the couple and the stories of the Christian tradition in order to understand more clearly their influence and to plan a wedding that symbolizes how they want to become married."[3] *Those who help prepare people for a second marriage need to be firm in their insistence that looking again at family of origin is essential for marrying again.* This emphasis on family of origin is less significant for people who marry again later in life after the death of a spouse. For them, their first family is the primary story that must be remembered in beginning a new narrative.

Preparation for a wedding of those marrying again should include also linking the stories of the first marriages of either or both partner to the stories from their families of origin. Previous marriages are part of the individual stories we bring to form a new family. They need to be told with candor and clarity. Story-telling is a central core of a relationship's identity. "Families tell stories in order to maintain their foundational beliefs, sustain their unique identity, and reaffirm their common values."[6] This is often conflicted in second marriages because of a desire to skip major, but unpleasant, chapters of one's history. And yet enabling couples to tell their stories to each other is at the heart of the pastoral task in all wedding preparation, and most certainly in the preparation of persons marrying again. The process of promising in a second marriage is restricted when the stories of a previous marriage cannot be rehearsed. Individuals marrying again struggle to leave behind the previous marriage, while at the same time recognizing the reality of that former relationship.

The second task in preparing couples for a second marriage is to explore the need for clear—but not fixed or impenetrable—boundaries between the generations or between members of the first family. As we have already noted, second marriages are by definition more permeable. When the boundaries are unclear, it is usually a sign that the individual who is remarrying has not sufficiently worked through the earlier marriage. We need to form a new community in which the roles are clear and the separation between the new family and the outside environment is well defined. When there are children involved in a second marriage, this becomes an essential task because a natural parent belongs to that outside environment. For this reason, marrying again is a double leaving; both one's family of origin and the first marriage. Preparation for marrying again may need to include a ritual process of reconciliation in order to leave behind the first relationship enough to marry again.

Forming new families requires careful attention to boundaries. It is no longer self-evident who belongs in our family and who does not. For instance, should the father of one's former husband who never had a grandson be allowed to take the son of a second marriage to a baseball game? Should you still send a birthday card to the sister of your former mother-in-law? We have seen remarried families in which the boundaries are so tightly drawn that children are not free to have solid relationships with both biological parents, or with friends from the old neighborhood. We have also seen families with boundaries so undefined that children had no real sense of belonging. When there is serious conflict because of the divorce, working out the relationship between clear boundaries and the right of access is a very important task. This is an issue for grandparents as well as parents in a second marriage.

The third task concerns mourning the losses that precede a second marriage. We cannot stress enough the need for grieving after a divorce occurs. That work of grieving will be enhanced if we can provide supportive social contexts in which the losses that accompany divorce are recognized. Within the Roman Catholic tradition, the sometimes grueling experience of annulment is a process that recognizes the pains of divorce.[7] For those who mourn the death of a spouse, the same kind of supportive network is necessary in order to do the work of grieving.

Grief is present at all weddings but it is a particularly problematic issue for those marrying again. The grief work for a marriage that ended is seldom finished before people marry again. Therefore, every second marriage is born in grief. In part, that is simply a recognition that we never fully stop grieving the loss of someone we love — whether that loss occurs through death or because of a divorce. The wedding ritual for a second marriage should help the couple and their communities grieve that which is to be no more, in preparation for that which is to come. Lingering grief is particularly present in children, whose omnipresent wishes that their parents not re-marry are confronted in the wedding, sometimes for the first time. Those wishes do not go away even after a parent has married a new partner. For everyone, including the children, the wedding ritual needs to give people permission to grieve what is no more in order to embrace what is to come. Acknowledging that grief is perhaps the most critical pastoral task.

Rituals for Marrying Again

Thinking about the wedding provides another opportunity for the couple to begin or continue healing unresolved issues from previous relationships. Planning the wedding is often a delicate process because it needs to combine family rituals from several sources which have been built up over time. The pastoral work of wedding preparation is a unique opportunity to help a couple begin the process of ritualizing their new life together in new and creative ways. The wedding of persons marrying again is complicated by the fact that it is not the couple's first encounter with the ritual.

> When we decided to marry after being divorced, our first thought was to have a small wedding, perhaps with our children and our parents present. But we weren't sure, so we talked with our pastor. He encouraged us to make it as complete a wedding as we could afford. So we made a wedding list and included people from both our former churches, our work colleagues, our book clubs and covenant groups, our friends (at least those who survived our divorces with us), and even my exercise class. The communion that was a central part of our wedding signaled a unity of purpose in joining us together.
>
> (David)

Much of the common wisdom regarding second marriages suggests that the wedding be small—often including only the couple who are marrying, a clergyperson, and the immediate family (parents and children). This practice and wisdom seems to have its grounding in the sense that a second marriage is an embarrassment, that the first wedding is really the one that calls for significant and elaborate celebration, and that to "make too much" of a second marriage borders on overstatement.

We believe that second weddings, at least as surely as first weddings, must be parabolic in character and communal in reality. It is very important that the significant communities of those marrying again surround the couple when they promise again. It is not necessary to create the parabolic character of a second marriage. The wedding itself is a sign of human finitude and human imperfection. We do need, however, to encourage the communal reality of a second marriage. Sometimes people prefer to marry again in secret in order to avoid shame or the awkwardness of complicated relationships that is almost inevitably present. Nevertheless, we envision weddings for people marrying again that bring together a wonderfully diverse multitude made up of the communities in which the couple belong. The gathering of all these supportive communities signals the awareness of, and the need for, the support of many others who *promised again* along with the marrying couple.

Since remarriage often involves bringing together families with complex new configurations, it is often helpful to celebrate this incorporation during the wedding ceremony itself. As family members are involved and recognized in the service, as they enter into the ritual of marriage with the couple, and as they begin to identify their *belonging* as this new family is formed, the act of promising again is expanded and new communities are formed.

There probably will be family members who find it difficult to enter into such a ceremony: they may feel loyalty to a former friend, parent, or child; they may have remaining hurt feelings about the death or divorce that preceded this marriage; they may have theological reasons for not participating; or they may in fact be caught between parents and unwittingly involved in a continuing battle leftover from a divorce. It is vital to honor the feelings of these persons. It is also important at the same time to offer an invitation for reconciliation with friends and family in order to be free to promise a new future.

The act of forming a new family, or any new covenant relationship, calls for an explicit reliance on God's creative activity in making and maintaining promises. The Christian service of marriage remembers and celebrates the presence of God as the "Guarantor of the Promise" at the same time that it acknowledges the limited nature of our ability to guarantee our own promises. A second marriage after a divorce is a sign that sin and guilt are part of the human condition. Even if the first marriage that ended with the death of a spouse was happy, there are vestiges of imperfection in our memory. When we include in the wedding service a recognition of forgiveness as an act of God, we strengthen the understanding of ultimate dependence on the providence of God in guaranteeing the promise for this new couple, and for this new family.

Those who marry again place their trust in the One who guarantees all promises, sometimes in the face of experience that points to the fragile nature of all human bonds. Those who marry again, like those who promise again, are bringing together their families of origin and the stories that make them family. But they are also bringing together the stories of families with whom they have formed other stories, making the progression geometric rather than one of simple addition. Promising again for people who have been married before is ultimately an act of faith in the face of apparent failure, faith in the One who stands behind all promises, both strong and weak.

6

TRANSFORMATION
IN MARRIAGE

CHANGE IS never easy. Neither is it always positive. It is, however, inevitable. Everything that lives changes. People change as they grow up and grow older. And because people change, families change as well. The family is never fixed. And marriage is a work in progress. It is always in the process of becoming something new. The natural transitions that occur during a family's history make change the norm rather than the exception. Most families move through these predictable moments with a normal amount of bumps and bruises, celebrating some changes, resisting others, and failing to note many other changes. When the change is unexpected or discontinuous enough to disrupt the balance in the relationship between wives and husbands, a crisis usually follows. And every crisis challenges a family's adaptability. It is generally agreed that the ability to adapt to change in creative and flexible ways is a mark of family vitality.

As families change, it is necessary to keep a balance between continuity and discontinuity. If the changes in a family's life are incremental enough, the perception of continuity predominates and the change goes unnoticed. If a family believes that maintaining continuity is necessary for stability, everybody stays in his or her place. Traditions remain untouched and the family is organized like a lifetime tour package. Families that devote time and energy to keeping things the same usually do so at a cost to one or more members. Most of the time, however, family change neither can be avoided nor eliminated. And it is usually disruptive enough to create a crisis of some kind. The ability to adapt to change is a central characteristic of effective family living. Adaptability, in turn, depends on mutuality and a willingness to sacrifice individual desires for the good of the familial relationship.

> Dierdre and I had both been married before. Neither of us had children. Before we were married, we talked extensively about my desire to have children. We knew it would be difficult because Dierdre had had back surgery in late adolescence. Even so, I thought we both wanted children. Without much warning, the frequency of sex declined dramatically shortly after we married. As we became less intimate, I raised the subject of children more often. What I could only sense is that Dierdre really did not want to have children but could not tell me. As a result, my love for Dierdre diminished. I felt abandoned by her in the commitment to have children. There was no possibility of recommitment on my part. I wanted a child more than I wanted the woman who would bear it.   (Kelvin)

This story is a poignant reminder that there are limits to adaptation. No person or system is infinitely flexible or capable of unlimited change. But without mutuality, it is even difficult to negotiate the different limits to change. Kelvin was unwilling to give up on his desire to have a child. We can only presume that adopting a child was unacceptable. Kelvin's desire to father a child was a circumstantial condition that turned the *primary* promise of their marriage into a contract. His unwillingness or inability to budge from that desire in order to adapt to new possibilities spelled doom for the marriage. Dierdre did not deal directly with her own limits either. Because this conflict existed early in the marriage, Dierdre and Kelvin probably were not emotionally bonded from the beginning. Promising in marriage is very difficult without effective communication and mutual adaptability.

Beyond Adaptation

Most of us are ambivalent about change. We fear it and desire it simultaneously. The inability to mourn is one of the major impediments to change in family living. Families that expect perfection also find change unsettling. When a family is dedicated to getting through life without any of its members having a divorce, an abortion, a psychological problem, or a failing grade, change that tarnishes its ideals threatens the family's purpose or well-being as well. This disorientation of purpose is a source of profound anxiety. Although we want to change, we often resist change out of fear. Even if the family transition is unavoidable and a good thing, we still resist change out of fear or because of the inability to mourn. For that reason, *homeostasis,* the determination to maintain equilibrium at all costs, frequently wins out over *morphogenesis,* the desire to make something new.

When we want change, there is another paradox that lingers. Our double-edged worry, even when we desire change, is that we have changed and yet have not changed. If we have changed, we are afraid that the familiar marital routine and predictable roles are gone forever. We may notice these changes in crowded datebooks, smaller food bills or dinners alone, different family roles, association with grandfathers and grandmothers in place of young friends. When we *think* we have adapted and changed, we are most vulnerable to nostalgia, so that the past will not be gone forever.

We are afraid, at the same time, that we have not really changed at all. That is the other face of this two-headed fear. This second fear is a hidden anxiety that in the end, everything will be as it has always been. Even if we cannot name it or do not know how to define it, what we long for is something new, not every day, but often. People change jobs, move to a new house, leave one marital partner for another, hoping for deeper change to occur. Deeper change does not usually happen, however, because it is a process that must unfold from within.

The fear that we have not changed is the other side of the longing to be transformed in an enduring way. This longing is clearly expressed in Paul's Letter to the Romans.

> We know that the whole creation has been groaning in labor pains until now; and not only the creation, but we ourselves, who have the first fruits of the Spirit, groan inwardly while we wait for adoption, the redemption of our bodies. (Rom. 8:22–23)

What we wait for is a new way of being. It is more than adaptation; it implies a new creative energy that flows from the center of an individual or a family. When that occurs, our terror of change becomes a desire and determination to grow.[1]

If we accept this desire to grow from within, adaptability alone is not enough to sustain family living. *Adaptation is not enough* because it is focused on the relationship between the present and the past. When adaptation turns to the future, we plan how we will cope with and act on an anticipated crisis. By contrast, the future is an active agent of change in the process of transformation. *Adaptation is not enough* when it aims to modify only external structures or patterns of interaction rather than internal dynamics. When the focus shifts to inward qualities and habits or the "soul of a marriage," the deeper change of transformation is needed. *Adaptation is not enough* because it is reactive rather than proactive. We may adjust and therefore survive, but our response is a reaction determined by immediate needs. Although our adapting is influenced by internal values and beliefs, it is not usually shaped by a larger vision that summons us to a new future. This vision is not necessarily an ideal to be achieved but a future to follow.

More Than Promising Again

Transformation moves beyond adaptation. It is also more than promising again. We have stated previously that promising again is a way of regularly renewing our commitments in accord with the changes that continue in our lives and our family relationships. Promising is an intentional, relational act that defines the self and limits the future. It is an act of mutuality because it presumes the willingness of two people to recognize each other as people of worth with particular gifts to give and a unique story to live. It is an act of faith because some new way of relating to another person is born out of crisis and chaos or the exercise of creative fidelity. Promising again is preferable to keeping promises because it recognizes that both the promise and the promise makers must be renewed and transformed in order to meet the challenges of change and keep faith with God's ongoing creative activity.

The metaphor of promising again has been used in this book in a variety of ways: (1) it is what couples must do when children leave home; (2) it is a way of thinking about remarriage after death or divorce; and (3) most important, promising again is a way of living in family and other communal relationships that acknowledges ongoing change in both the promise and the promisors. Mutuality and adaptability make it easier for all families to live through change. The capacity to change in a deeper, more enduring sense, however, is grounded in a belief that the continuity of a family is in God's ongoing creation. Paradoxically, families that accept change as inevitable are more open to what God is making new and more willing to accept deeper change beyond adaptation or promising again. Transformation, as change beyond adaptation, is necessary for the future of family living. This understanding of transformation is similar to what family therapists have described as the change of change.[2] It presumes the possibility of a radically different way of perceiving, thinking, or interacting within a family.

Like promising again, transformation often occurs at moments of radical discontinuity. Rosemary Haughton, a Roman Catholic theologian, suggests that "transformation is the timeless occurrence to which all previous and succeeding circumstances are totally irrelevant."[3] Haughton's approach to transformation fits with our understanding of family living today precisely because discontinuity is so common, even when marriages endure. Promising again may not be enough to sustain relationships throughout the turbulence of the present time. Something like transformation is required.

> Both Gilbert and I have been involved in demanding careers since before the marriage began. Those commitments to our jobs did not diminish when our children were born. We simply added parenting tasks to an already stressful existence. After we had children, our family life would overload about every six months and we would renegotiate the distribution of household responsibilities. By our tenth wedding anniversary, we had become crabby strangers in our own home, too exhausted for sex, and fearfully distant from our children. What we needed to change, we both agreed, was obvious and yet it seemed impossible. (Sandra)

Promising again is necessary for couples like Gilbert and Sandra because the *secondary* promises that form the character of their marital bond have eroded or have been severely challenged by stress. Gilbert and Sandra needed to refurbish the *primary* promise. It was the change that seemed obvious but impossible. Promising again is a prelude to transformation because it promotes enough commitment that a wife and husband are willing to stay in the covenant. Because they had retained a bond of mutual regard, Gilbert and Sandra could discover their deeper longings for the sake of transformation. This way of transforming the soul of a marriage happens more slowly and from the inside out. It is God's new creation of fidelity and hope in the midst of alienation and despair.

Transformative Change

Our proposal is this: *Transformation is necessary in order that the changes in marriage and family living will be deep enough and sturdy enough to endure the rigors of modern family living.* Systemic adaptation helps a couple deal with stress-producing changes that occur at the level of time-limited, situational or *tertiary* promises. Promising again and again keeps us connected as partners in the covenant of marriage. We are particularly aware of the fragility of promising again when the ordinary crises of being married are combined with the stress of modern living. In light of that stress, transformation is necessary in order to provide a radical shift in the self-understanding and strategies of persons and families. Transformative change unites the soul of a marriage with a longing for the new thing God is doing.

> One of Martha's favorite pastimes was rearranging the living room. At least once a month, I could expect to come home from work and find the furniture moved. Most of the time I recognized the place. Sometimes, however, it seemed as if I had wandered into another house. I might have wished for a little more stability, but I tolerated it as an outlet for Martha's creativity. I was not prepared for the day when I came home and all the furniture and Martha were gone. I must have missed the message.　　　　　　　　　　　　　　　　　　　　(Ronald)

Ronald thought his adaptive tolerance of Martha's creative furniture moving was sufficient. He discovered too late that it was not. He might have said that he had been faithful in his promises to Martha. Even that was not sufficient. Transformation is more than rearranging the furniture in the living room or allowing it to happen. It is the discovery of the meaning of living in the family house in relationship to the family's self-understanding. We do not know Martha's reasons for leaving. We can only guess that her sudden and seemingly revolutionary act was necessary because no other change was enough.

The theme of transformation makes at least six contributions to our understanding of how couples like Ronald and Martha must change to endure. First, transformation does not presume the resolution of the paradoxical nature of family living. It is, in fact, a profound expression of the centrality of paradox in human life. Second, both individuals and families are a unique unity of form and spirit. Perfect arrangements of furniture or a well-organized family structure are not enough. Adaptation of family form must be balanced by the transformation of a family's spirit.

Third, transformation is a theological way of recognizing discontinuous change throughout the family life cycle. It acknowledges the power of God's grace to transform despite either the chaos or the sameness of our lives. Fourth, transformation is something that happens to us as well as something we do. We are being transformed, sometimes even when we do not know it. Couples who understand this passive, sometimes unrecognized, aspect of transformation will be better prepared to wait for change. Fifth, the future of a family is as important as its past. Both are active agents of change in the present. However, just as with all communities of people, families will perish if they have no vision.

Finally, transformation presumes the interconnectedness of all things. Throughout this series we have been working on the reciprocity of systemic change and individual change, between social and personal transformation. This effort is linked to a larger and older debate about the relationship between individual and social change, between working to change social systems and seeking to transform individuals who will create hospitable and just environments. That debate is usually dictated by linear thinking in which one thing precedes another, and the second follows as a consequence of the first. The idea of circular causality, one of the theoretical foundations of family systems' thinking, alters the question. Which comes first, social or individual transformation, is a moot point. Both are necessary and each participates in the transformation of the other.

Understanding Transformation

Although it is possible to understand transformation as a secular reality, we use it here in its distinctly Christian sense. There are at least two ways of understanding transformation theologically. One emphasizes the necessity of conversion as the normative form of change while the other stresses the formative aspect of human or spiritual growth. In reality, both are necessary for the experience of transformation. However, most would agree that changes in family living must be both immediate and long-term, as well as personal and social, in order to be deep enough to make a difference. What we say, therefore, about transformative change in marriage must be as paradoxical as the human nature it seeks to redeem.

Transformation Is Human Work and the Work of God

When the focus is on personal transformation, the passive voice is often used. The phrase *being transformed* suggests that it is something that happens to us. We do not transform ourselves, either as individuals or as families. What we communicate with the passive voice is that transformation is the work of God in human life. We may experience this gift of God's grace in Christ Jesus in our homes. The family is a place where transformation may occur "in the moment of self-surrender to love. . . . For each one, alone, is helpless, and only the knowledge of *being loved* has the power to set free into faith."[4] What transforms is this gift of *being loved* by someone who knows us as fully as wives and husbands can come to know one another. We cannot love each other in marriage in this way solely from within ourselves. Even when we understand transformation as human work, it is empowered and gifted by God.

> In the twenty-second year of our marriage, for reasons I still do not fully understand, my husband Merton became intensely jealous and accused me (falsely) of having an affair with one of his high school friends. Both of our children had left home and I was ready for something new in our relationship. But not jealousy. I continued to love Merton but I could not bear *not* being loved. I thought about leaving several times. When I was at my wits end with loneliness, Merton decided to attend a men's retreat sponsored by our church on "David of Old, Men of Today." When he came home, it was clear that something had changed. The jealousy disappeared as suddenly and mysteriously as it began. Merton was also easier to love than before. (Sue)

The story of Merton and Sue illustrates many aspects of transformation. It is something we do and it is something that happens to us. It is an identifiable process and it is a mystery. Although Merton did not report an experience of God's transforming love, it was easier for him to be loved after the retreat. Something had changed in him that altered his attitude toward Sue and the marriage as well.

Although we cannot transform ourselves, we are commanded to be agents of transformation of others, in our homes as well as in our neighborhoods. Loving our neighbor is not optional. For many people, the nearest neighbor is one's parent, child, wife, or husband. To be agents of transformation is intentional soul work that affects the whole of one's being and compels us to act for our neighbor.

Transformation Is both Personal and Social

The work of adaptation in families is, we suggest, largely social or systemic in nature. It is about how we change the structures, rules, or rituals of a family to make it a more hospitable place in which to live.

When this is possible, the family becomes a community-creating community. Societies must keep changing also in order to be friendly to families that comprise them. We often use the language of transformation in reference to the change we hope to effect in societies, neighborhoods, and churches in which we live. It is less common, however, to refer to the transformation of families.

Personal transformation is more difficult to discuss because it is internal more than external, dispositional as well as behavioral. Rosemary Haughton observes that transformation happens when we are tending toward conversion. We lean so that we can fall. "For when transformation occurs it transforms the whole personality in so far as it is aware of itself—that is, in so far as it has reached full definition as personal."[5] Transformation is total. Yet all the same, human transformation is beyond our strenuous efforts to be moral.

There are obscure motives and hidden needs that continue to impede our desire for transformation. Our conscious striving to improve our moral life needs to be transformed into the desire to love and be loved. In this, we encounter a fundamental paradox of struggle and surrender. Personal transformation begins when we surrender our work to God. Transformative change in families is a paradoxical process of human work *and* the work of God that bridges social and individual transformation.

Transformation Re-forms the Past without Rejecting It

This is an important understanding of transformation as it occurs in family living, because it allows discontinuity and continuity to be paradoxically linked in transformation. "Unlike a conversion, a transformation does not require a rejection or negation of the past or previously held values. Instead, a transformation involves a new perception, re-cognition, of the past."[6] This line from a definition of transformation by biblical theologian Beverly Roberts Gavanta contrasts with the radical discontinuity in Rosemary Haughton's definition. Both are true. And for the sake of deepening marital covenants, both *must* be true. We do not remember the initial promise in marriage just to keep it: we remember this promise in order to renew and redefine it for the sake of a new future. Yet the initial promise must be remembered. The potential for continuity is in the remembering.

The continuity is also in changing. That is the saving paradox for family living. The emphasis is on the continual transformation of the family as it discovers and forms new relationships within itself, with others, and with God. The late Anglican practical theologian Romney

M. Moseley expands this concept "beyond its strictly biological roots as a process of adaptation to the environment, [and] to emphasize *constant change* over adaptation."[7] The process of transformation is always unfinished. It is living with struggle and surrender. The hardest part of living with Christ, Moseley says, "is to let God's self-emptying love in Christ become for us a way of loving God and one another."[8]

> Denise and I had only been married for a short time when both my parents died, we moved to another city, and I became interested in religion again. We also discovered then we could not have children. We needed the help of a marriage counselor to hurdle those changes in a constructive way. From then until now, although we have moved several more times, our lives have remained relatively constant. Within the last year, however, we celebrated our twenty-fifth wedding anniversary, the corporation I work for downsized everything including my job, and Denise was made department head at her school of nursing. As a result, Denise is now the primary breadwinner in the marriage. Those changes in the workplace have been harder on the marriage than we first thought. Sometimes I think work is exceedingly important for both of us because we do not have children. We do not have children leaving home but we need to renew our promises to one another in light of these role changes in the marital bond.   (Harry)

What Denise and Harry have discovered after twenty-five years of marriage is that even when things stay the same, change is constant. They have also learned that there is no permanent resolution of conflict at the end of transformation. Instead, as Moseley invites us, we need to move purposely and vigorously into "the paradox of struggle and surrender, fulfillment and emptiness . . . between the is and ought, between the selves that we are and the selves that we ought to be."[9] The aim of transformation is not stability that we hope will not change. It is faithfulness enough to remain in those covenants like marriage that live the paradox. That is why promising again is the prelude to transformation. We live *with* people we love. We live *by* making temporary truces. We live *toward* an uncertain future. Becoming and being married are not fixed on one promise.

Enabling Transformation in Marriage

Although we do not make transformation happen, we are responsible for creating the kind of environment in which it is more likely to occur. What are the conditions that are most likely to enhance the kind of transformation in marriage that enables change to endure? Rosemary Haughton creatively uses the *encounter* of marriage to develop the necessary paradoxical relationship between formation and transformation for family living. According to Haughton, formation and transformation are related in reciprocal ways in marriage. "The opportunity for a transforming breakthrough, the chance to make a decision for love, only occurs because the previous formation has shaped a personality inclined to love."[10] This statement points to a dilemma facing families today. People marry and have children without being adequately formed for family living. Or the way they have been formed for family is not "inclined to love." In these instances, the first step of transformation in marriage is for husbands and wives to turn toward one another and lean into love. This is most likely to happen if the people entering the marital process understand promising to include loyalty, service, devotion, and *tending toward the other.*

Leaving home and becoming married are both aspects of family living in which formation is primary. Separating from the home of one's origin culminates a process of identity formation by granting an individual new status in his or her family. It is also the process by which people are formed with varying degrees of personal authority. The task of becoming married is to form a bond that recognizes the legacies of each spouse, yet has its own identity. It is a process of moving from an "I" to a "we" without losing the autonomy of the "I." The final aim of this process, as it is suggested in the book in this series, *Becoming Married,* is to be formed into a "covenant of abiding seriousness." This determination to recognize the other with abiding seriousness is one of the *secondary* promises that we noted in chapter 1.

It is often obvious when people are not prepared for marriage or when couples have gone as far as they can in their version of being married. This does not necessarily mean that something is bad or wrong in the relationship, but that what worked once no longer works. From that perspective, we can understand how *transformation must break through when formation breaks down.* Transformation depends, Haughton rightly insists, "on previous formation, for it is only because they have the courage and 'sense of direction' to keep turned toward each other that the lovers can experience their conflict as forming and transforming."[11]

Aunt Marian and Uncle Bill celebrated their fiftieth wedding anniversary at St. Boniface Church just before I was married. The entire extended family and many friends were there to celebrate with them. Aunt Marian and Uncle Bill always had a way of bringing people together. Their public recommitment to each other and to being married was a hopeful sign for me. It was also a moment of sadness for Marian and Bill because they never had children. What I remember most about that celebration were the stories that people told about their generosity. The image of Uncle Bill and Aunt Marian on that day was a powerful lesson for me at the beginning of my marriage.

(Cynthia)

Formation for marriage occurs in formal settings as we teach about the meaning of marriage. That the church is engaged in catechesis with young people about marriage is a recognition of this need for formation. It happens also in informal ways as we observe the marriages of those we respect or we celebrate the life together of family members. Cynthia's story of Aunt Marian and Uncle Bill is an instance of informal formation for being married.

Haughton believes that transformation is also the release of power in communities that live toward conversion. To live toward conversion means to be open to ongoing change. This sense of tending toward change is absolutely essential if transformation is to occur. What that means in marriage is that two people live together, each tending toward the other. It is this vision of life that makes it possible for quite sane people to consider getting married. In his reflections on Martin Buber's "I-Thou," English theologian Nicholas Lash insists that community can only *happen* in a time like ours when people turn toward relation. "But if conversion, the turn to relation, needs therefore to occur again, if 'personal' existence has to struggle, again and again, to win through over 'ego-tism,' this will only happen if memory of its possibility, the memory of its past occurrence, is kept alive."[12] The moment of meeting occurs and passes. But it occurs because we are *tending toward* its occurrence.

These observations by Lash about conversion as the turn toward relation add a significant dimension to our understanding of what makes transformation possible. We are willing to turn *again* toward the other in marriage because there is a memory of some time when the relationship was bonded by love. Couples need to believe that the occurrence of community they remember in their marriage was a "particular enactment of universal possibility."[13] It was not a fluke; it could happen again. Memory then becomes hope. And hope for genuine meeting again in some future time keeps us turning toward the other.

Since human beings and human communities are finite and flawed, repentance or metanoia, according to Haughton, comes before transformation in order that something new will be formed. This is the hardest statement of all. There is no transformation without forgiveness, and the possibility of forgiveness in marriage depends on repentance. Haughton believes that transformation begins with repentance. We repent of ways we have hurt our spouse. We also turn aside from all efforts to be virtuous. Presuming to be righteous is a barrier to forgiveness in marriage. We move from repentance to the "dissolution of all that ordinary people value in themselves or others."[14] Transformation is very costly. We know that from the cross. We also know it from family living. The love that transforms is a surrender without any knowledge of what may come of it.

> Over the years, I had become dissatisfied both with myself and our marriage. I did not know who I was. My husband was also a stranger. I suspect that my husband Randell had felt the same way because of the way he spent more time at work than with me. Neither of us make sudden decisions. So it is not surprising that without discussion, we concluded that we did not have sufficient reason to leave the marriage. Each of us went on a quest for what we personally needed. Randell worked his quest out in the workplace. I returned to the faith of my childhood and found acceptance, comfort, and love. Many people walked with me, sharing their experiences, offering words of wisdom, pointing to another vision. I came to the realization that my conceptions about who I thought I was and who I wanted to be, and who I thought Randell was and what I wanted my marriage to be *all had to die* so that God could transform me and Randell and recreate the marriage. It was a journey that took ten years. Our marriage is now more than I ever dreamed possible. The transformation is reflected in three changes in our relationship: it is more playful, more honest, and more mutual. (Jessica)

What is most striking about Jessica's story is her willingness to let the old marital bond with Randell die so that something new might come to be. It was a risky wager. It was, however, consistent with what Haughton has identified as the center of transformation.

What she is proposing may seem more radical and discontinuous than most people in marriage are prepared for. It is, however, the fundamental Christian paradox applied to family living. In order to live, we have to die.

The love given in marriage involves a sort of death, for it is a giving without hope of return. The lover dies in this love. But receiving this love is also a death. We do not know what will happen to us because of the love we receive. "So both in giving and receiving love there is *obedience,* a surrender to the command to love of which each is aware through the other. *Each* is both a giver of love, which involves a dying, and a receiver of love, to which the response is also dying. . . . And out of this death a *new life* is born, one which is shared."[15] Transformation occurs in this moment of self-surrender to love. Something new is possible in marriage when two people yield control in order to be loved. And when we surrender to the mutuality of being loved, we are also receptive to the transforming love of God.

According to Haughton, transformation is also an intentional act. All communities, "have to become on-purpose. . . . People marry on purpose, but Cupid's inability to shoot straight is notorious . . . and even under the guidance of the oracles of family planning the advent of children into a family is wildly accidental."[16] The process of becoming married begins with an intentional act. It has been important for the Christian community since the Reformation era, to insist on intentionality as a way of honoring the freedom to choose whom one marries. In the end, however, the family is a thoroughly random, sometimes wildly unlikely, collection of people. The family's task is to make a community "on-purpose" from this odd assembly. The family is, therefore, always a community-making community. In that sense, becoming married is itself an act of transformation.

For Haughton, transformation affects the whole personality insofar as it is aware of itself. This presses the question of self-awareness. Transformation is not just an intellectual process. We are invited to discover deeper dimensions of living and being married that often are outside our awareness. We do not change our covenants of marriage by reason alone. Family living is too paradoxical. If it is true that we are a mystery to ourselves, then marriage and family living is the multiplication of mystery. Sometimes the most difficult choice we have to make in a marriage is whether we are willing to live with questions for which there are no answers.

How Transformation Happens

Transformation is human work as well as God's work. Our first task is to create the kind of environment in which transformation is most likely to happen. The second is to foster ways of living in families that promote transformation. We suggest five strategies that could lead to deeper and enduring change: discerning deeper metaphors, practicing self-transcending love, understanding our obligations, saying the other side, and living with mystery. Don S. Browning writes about two of these strategies under the heading of practical moral rationality. "When a transformation is effected at the higher levels of practical thinking—the visional and obligational—and is both genuine and deep, we are likely to call this a *conversion*."[17] We agree and would go even deeper. It is imperative for couples to examine the metaphors and obligations that inform their life together in order to transform their interactional system for the sake of enduring change.

Discerning Deeper Metaphors

The purpose of discerning deeper metaphors is to discover the operative beliefs that govern a couple's interaction. The purpose of discerning deeper metaphors is to formulate a story that allows for a new future. Transformation is most likely to occur in marriage when the marital pair can imagine a new narrative that transcends the old, sometimes painful, often constricting marital story. The aim of discerning the deeper metaphors, then, is the transformation of imagination.

When husbands and wives fight, it is usually *not* about the deep metaphors of life. It is usually about power and loyalty and unmet expectations for intimacy. Nor is the conflict cast in philosophical categories. Yet, sooner or later, the fight focuses on competing or conflicting convictions and values. How the toilet should be cleaned or the car repaired are about how we think the world should be ordered. More often than not, these deep metaphors exist outside our awareness. In the middle of the conflict, we may know for certain that something is wrong, but we are hard-pressed to say why. We may be absolutely determined that our way to raise children is right, but we are a little vague about our rationale.

> When I left the family farm to enter law school, I was surprised by my father's opposition. He regarded my desire to become a lawyer as an impossible dream. Much later, I learned that I had challenged a deeper family metaphor: simplicity. I made that discovery when my wife and I were about to buy the house that both of us had dreamed of owning. All of a sudden, for reasons unknown to me at the time, I balked. I knew that my

resistance was not rational but I did not know why. In conversations with a marriage counselor, I remembered a saying of my mother to which my father would always concur: "We are simple people; we better stay where we are." Buying the house was the second time I was violating the family belief in simplicity.

(Mario)

Mario's story is a compelling illustration of the way in which the deeper metaphors of our lives often have power and influence outside our awareness. We do not know from the story whether identifying the deeper family metaphor was enough to free Mario from its claims. Simply naming the governing metaphors does not automatically transform them. Even so, we need to be aware that the old storyline has often been tarnished by unmet expectations, broken promises, hurtful arguments, bittersweet memories, unforgettable violence, willful deceptions, and other instances of human sinfulness in marriage. These are the things that are often remembered whenever troubled couples tell their story. It is difficult for troubled couples to imagine beyond the present. Family therapist Donald S. Williamson has used the evocative phrase "remembering a different future" to describe this process. We need to be able to reconstruct the story of our past in the present so that new possibilities for a different future are imaginable.[18]

Discerning the deeper metaphors in a marriage helps us live with the daily promises we make in two ways that are paradoxically connected: (1) We are better able to distinguish between the big issues and the little things in family living. Little things often accumulate in a marital relationsip but they are *still little things*. When we are clear about the deeper values that are at the center of our life together, we may forget little things that are not worth fighting for; and (2) It is the little things that count in marriage. They add to the rhythms of a marriage. When little things accumulate, they ultimately reflect back on the *primary* promise to love, honor, and cherish. When little things challenge the *primary* promise, couples need to rethink the deep metaphors that govern their relationship.

Changing the deep metaphors of our lives in order to imagine a different future can be a complex and emotionally charged process. It cannot be done simply by fiat or by reason. It begins by discerning the values that govern the present and acknowledging the power of family myths that order daily living. More often than not, a family determines to develop a new story without consciously deciding to live according to a new set of values or intentionally challenging the deeper metaphors. Only later, the family may discover that the new story reinforces the beliefs that got them into trouble in the first place. Sometimes, however, the old metaphors are challenged directly and a new narrative is proposed. When a new narrative is proposed, it needs to be paradoxical enough to embrace the experience of married life today. It also must be comprehensive enough to contain the contradictions of marriage and family living that cannot be resolved.

In order to change a family narrative, couples need to recover and reaffirm their first dream of being a family—a dream that has been lost and forgotten in the turmoil of their life together. In another volume in this series, *Becoming Married,* it was suggested that couples develop a theme for the wedding, such as hospitality or justice, that reflects a vision of the kind of family they intend. In that sense, the wedding is a *proleptic event* because it anticipates a future and embodies a vision of that future in the present moment. That vision of our family's future is certainly filled with dreams that have their origins in both the present and the past. Even if those dreams were not formulated explicitly, they still live on in the memory of expectations. The focus should be on the original vision, not the failure to fulfill it. It is another way of remembering a different future.

From the perspective of faith, the future we envision is formed by the promises of God. Ted Peters, in his book on *God—The World's Future,* suggests that "proleptic consciousness" is an awareness of the future based on "God's promise and upon faith in God's faithfulness."[19] That promise enables us to overcome anxiety about the present by assuring the future, "especially a future that is not stuck by the precedents of the past. To be is to have a future. To lose one's future and have only a past is to die."[20] Having a vision of the future is crucial for transformation. When we refer to *being transformed* in the passive voice, we mean, in part, that we are being acted upon in the present by God's promised future.

Self-Transcending Love

The willingness to compromise, we have said, is part of promising again. Compromise is necessary because people change. We seldom marry the person we thought we were marrying, and the person with whom we promise again is not the same person to whom we made the initial promise. We also have to compromise whenever we want more than we can afford or have time for. And mutual compromise is necessary for a relationship to be just. There are no perfect solutions or answers to anything in marriage. We need to be prepared to sacrifice, to give up something in order to sustain compromise in family living. This is what we mean when we say that self-transcending love, the ability to transcend one's own desires or needs for the common good, makes transformation possible.

Sacrificial loving comes before compromise in marriage. Each partner in the marital bond must be willing to sacrifice for the common good of the marriage. Charles Handy has labeled this concern for the common good "trinitarian, or third angle thinking," always looking for another approach or a third angle that makes compromise possible. He says, "We need to find a common cause, one that justifies some personal sacrifice by both parties for a greater common good."[21] When we say that our marriage sustains our life, we are engaging in "trinitarian thinking." When we say that marital love is a religious vocation that is a mirror of Christ's love for the church, we have added a "third angle" to being married that invites each spouse to look beyond personal needs and desires for the sake of the common good.

Sacrificial love, however, is not the only mode of self-transcending love in family living. The attraction that begins a relationship is mostly erotic. Authentic *eros*-love in marriage links self-interest and the yearning for happiness with a desire for intimacy. It is a way of loving in marriage that needs to be celebrated and nurtured. Most marriages suffer from too little rather than too much erotic loving. Our task in marriage is to transform erotic love rather than to reject it. Friendship is another form of love that sustains families. It is a way wives and husbands love one another in which love of the other and love of the self find mutual expression. Friendship is what parents and children hope to achieve on the other side of launching and leaving home.

The Roman Catholic tradition adds another understanding of loving that has consequences for family living. It stresses *caritas* as a synthesis of human love from the self and the divine love given in Jesus Christ. In *caritas,* the self is affirmed, confirmed, and transformed by God's gift of love. Loving is understood as equal regard in which the optimal development of each person is honored. When this ethic of love is applied to marriage, it means that personal development counts equally with development for my spouse. Love as equal regard means that we are to take our own needs and interests *and* the needs and interests of the neighbor (in this case understood as family) with equal seriousness.[22] Authentic striving for self-fulfillment and authentic striving for the common good are both respected and enhanced. Human fulfillment *and* mutuality are possible because of self-transcendence which is sustained by God's love. Modern understandings of intimacy lend support to the idea that creativity and self-fulfillment are legitimate and enriching desires of the human spirit. The kind of *creative fidelity* that we have been developing in this book presumes that working for a better self is part of marital faithfulness.

We know clearly from all the troubles of being married that this ideal of equal regard does not always work. We do not always recognize that the needs and interests of spouse or children are of equal importance. One solution to this dilemma is to include self-sacrifice as a way of restoring mutuality that has been disrupted by human selfishness. Sacrificial love becomes necessary only when the willingness to compromise (for the sake of equal regard) has failed. By itself, sacrificial loving in the family is also an impossible ideal that must be corrected by equal regard lest one person become the primary compromiser.

Both self-fulfillment and the discipline of sacrificial loving need to be informed by the reality of authentic, consistent, and lasting self-transcendence, if transformation is to occur.[23] We need to discern the deeper values and metaphors of both self-fulfillment and self-sacrifice. For that reason, self-transcendence and transformation must be together for the sake of intimacy in family living.

Understanding Our Obligations

Finding a balance between what we must do, what we could do, and what we would like to do is an ongoing human dilemma. Sometimes we cast this dilemma in terms of duty and responsibility. Duty relates to the basic core of our obligations, about what we must do in relation to work and family. There was a time when doing our duty took most of our time. Today, duties and obligations are often debated, negotiated, and renegotiated at the level of *tertiary* promises. Still, for some families, doing what must be done to make enough to feed and clothe a family takes most of their time. For those families, there is no life beyond the core of duty. Ideally, however, our ultimate responsibility in life reaches beyond the bounds of duty, to live up to our full potential. Responsibility always extends beyond duty.

It is seldom easy to maintain a balance between work and family, between necessity and choice. Keeping that balance is the reason why *tertiary* promises must be reviewed and renewed often. Moreover, how families arrive at that balance is one indication of the significance of justice in the deeper metaphors that govern their functioning. Are family obligations something mutually agreed upon and equally shared? Does each partner in the marriage have equal freedom to explore gifts and responsibilities beyond those obligations? Is the family as a whole able to distinguish between its obligations to each other and to the wider community? Without clear boundaries, a family is easily oppressed by guilt. Enough is never enough.

The life-cycle moment of launching children is a time when couples need to reconsider the relationship between duty and responsibility because there are fewer obligations in the family and more freedom to pursue the fulfillment of individual gifts and interests. When we revisit the leaving-home agenda, we need to be clear why we are willing to fulfill some family obligations and not others. This time around, the issue of leaving home is not so much about autonomy or personal authority as it is about parental accountability. When parents understand their obligations to children in a new way, their own sense of duty may diminish.

Parents who promise again while aging parents are still alive find themselves in a particularly difficult situation of competing loyalties and obligations. They are torn between their obligations to aging parents and their perceived obligations to young adult children. In many traditional cultures, the question of obligation is moot. The first loyalty is to one's parents until they die. The eldest son or daughter cares for the parents, even if he or she is married with children and has another set of obligations. The child designated by family tradition or cultural expectations to care for elderly parents may never marry, thus avoiding the conflict of obligations that inevitably occurs.

Saying the Other Side

The ultimate mystery of family living is a paradox. Throughout this series of books, we have attempted to show that families remain vital and open to change when they keep alive the separate/together paradox, which can be expressed as follows:

— We love our children by letting them go.
— We celebrate community by honoring autonomy.
— We leave home to make a home.

— We long for a home with a room of our own.

— We find it easier to be married if we can be alone.

— We have formed a good marriage when each spouse appoints the other as guardian of his or her solitude.

— We are fortunate when the vitality of family living is shaped by the rhythms of venturing and abiding.

— We can be in a committed relationship even though fidelity is both a gift and a surprise.

— We find life, ultimately, by losing it.

We regularly risk overlooking the deeper truths of life because of our desire to eliminate contradiction. When we make family living only a problem to be solved, we miss the paradox and the mystery. Coping with family change and enhancing transformation ultimately requires two paradoxically related tasks. We need to *remember* the former things in order to mourn the losses that accompany change. We need to *forget* the former things so that we can see and perceive the new thing that God is doing in our lives and in our families.

In each of these volumes, it has been suggested that "saying the other side" is a necessary pastoral strategy in order to keep paradox alive. Most of us don't like paradox. It is messy, chaotic, troublesome, and too much like fuzzy-mindedness. The mother of a friend of ours would regularly say, "I said 'maybe' and that's final!" Most of us avoid contradictions when we can. It is awkward always having to say two things, too much like permanently walking a tightrope or speaking with "forked tongue" or straddling two paths. Because of this inclination to avoid contradiction, we need to "say the other side" in pastoral conversations with couples and families in order to keep paradox alive.

When this framework is used by those who minister with couples in conflict, "saying the other side" is a pastoral intervention that will only work if a solid empathic bond has been established with both partners in the marriage. As already noted, we are emotionally wedded to our deep metaphors and preferred absolutes, even when we don't know fully what they mean. Helpers need to listen carefully, respond empathically, and take seriously the prevailing narrative or operational belief system *before* suggesting very gently the possibility of another side to the story.

The fact that there are at least two sides to a story already complicates this method of pastoral conversation with couples when their marriage is troubled. Each partner has a story of his or her own individual journey within the context of the marriage. When working with couples, "saying the other side" means making sure that each version of the marriage story is told and heard. The pastoral task is to help the couple discover a new narrative that transcends the destructive story they continue to live and tell. At the same time, it is necessary to listen to the journies of individual growth. *Creative fidelity*, as we have defined it, takes all three stories seriously in the light of the larger Christian story: each individual's own story and the story of their marriage.

When "saying the other side" is a discipline for couples in their conversations about their life together, it must begin with a shared conviction that *there is another side*. If transformation is to occur, there is no room for absolutizing. One can always hear two things, both of which are equally valid. And maybe both are true. "Saying the other side" is a useful way of making sure that everyone's voice is heard. It is a reminder of the ongoing discipline of empathy that is needed for marriage today. It can be a liberating method, however, only if everyone agrees that first, the deepest truths of life and faith are to be found in paradox, and second, that learning to live with contradiction and paradox is necessary for family well-being. We agree with Rosemary Haughton when she suggests that embracing ambiguity "brings about the transformation which is faith."[24]

Living the Mystery

Paradox is about mystery. Learning to acknowledge (if not embrace) contradiction as part of family living is one way to live that mystery. How and why and when transformation occurs in marriage is also a mystery. In an essay written in 1942 titled "The Mystery of the Family," the French Catholic philosopher Gabriel Marcel wrote that there is a deep similarity between the union of the soul and body and the mystery of the family. "It is in this very definite sense that the family is a mystery, and it is for this reason that we cannot properly and without confusion treat it simply as a question to be solved."[25]

It is a mystery how any one of us comes to be who we are out of the succession of historical processes we identify as our lineage. We may locate certain psychological dispositions or physical characteristics with our family origins, but each person is a unique creation of God. That is a mystery. How we chose the one we love or love the one that is chosen is another imponderable. How the gift of children fills a family with energy when they come and emptiness when they leave is a small sign of the paradoxical mystery of life and death. The purpose of evoking the mystery of the family, according to Marcel, is "far less to attempt to resolve a problem than to try to recapture a reality and awaken the soul to its presence."[26]

Promising again is not a problem to be solved but a mystery to be experienced. We have described the characteristics of promising. We have also noted the kinds of crises that make promising again necessary. We have identified the impediments that inhibit promising. And we have nuanced the general and particular aspects of promising again at various moments in the life cycle of a marriage and after divorce or the death of a spouse.

Finally, however, the experience of promising again takes us beyond the end we imagined. Even the promise, as T. S. Eliot has reminded us, is altered in its fulfillment. That is the ultimate paradox of promising in marriage. The expectations of being married from our wedding day are broken when they are fulfilled. For that reason, it is not enough that we keep promises. Instead, we continue promising again and again. We don't always know how or why people change and marriages are transformed. Even so, we continue to make new promises in hope. Hope for the future of marriage is the final secret of promising. This hope cannot be separated from either our tending toward one another or God's tending toward us. When hope is part of the marital bond, there are possibilities even in the toughest situations. Whenever we promise again as part of family living, we participate in this mystery of fidelity and hope.

NOTES

Introduction

1. John H. Snow, *On Pilgrimage* (New York: Seabury Press, 1971), 143.

2. Judith S. Wallerstein and Sandra Blakeslee, *The Good Marriage: How and Why Love Lasts* (Boston: Houghton Mifflin Co., 1995), 269.

3. *Marriage in America: A Report to the Nation* (New York: Institute for American Values, 1995), 3.

4. Wallerstein and Blakeslee, *The Good Marriage,* 27–28.

5. Sonya Rhodes, D.S.W., with Joleen Wilson, *Surviving Family Life: The Seven Crises of Living Together* (New York: G.P. Putnam's Sons, 1981), 16. There are a variety of books that suggest a similar theme. Couples can make marriage last by enduring predictable crises or understanding and managing the many marriages—and divorces—in every committed relationship. See Mel Krantzler and Patricia B. Krantzler, *The Seven Marriages of Your Marriage* (San Francisco: HarperCollins, 1992).

6. Charles Handy, *The Age of Paradox* (Boston: Harvard Business School Press, 1994), 13.

Chapter 1. The Gift of Promising

1. Rodney J. Hunter, "Commitment," in *Dictionary of Pastoral Care and Counseling* (Nashville: Abingdon Press, 1990), 195–97. See also J. C. Haughey, "Promising," Ibid., 960–62.

2. Louis B. Smedes, *Caring and Commitment: Learning to Live the Love We Promise* (San Francisco: Harper & Row, 1989), 39.

3. T. S. Eliot, "Four Quartets: Little Gidding," *Collected Poems and Plays 1909–1962* (San Diego, Calif.: Harcourt, Brace & Co., 1963), 139.

4. Gabriel Marcel, *Creative Fidelity,* trans. by Robert Rosthal (New York: Farrar, Straus & Co., 1964), 153.

5. Margaret A. Farley, *Personal Commitments: Beginning, Keeping, Changing* (San Francisco: Harper & Row, 1986).

6. Ibid., 6.

7. Sam Keen, quoted in William Sloan Coffin, *The Courage to Love* (San Francisco: Harper & Row, 1984).

8. Farley, *Personal Commitments,* 19.

9. Marcel, *Creative Fidelity,* 158. "All I have the right to affirm is that it certainly seems to me that my feeling or inner disposition cannot change . . . but I can't be sure of it. It is then impossible for me to declare: I swear that my inner disposition will not change. This immutability no longer is the object of my allegiance," ibid.

10. Salvador Minuchin and Michael P. Nichols, "The Unspoken Contract," *Networker,* vol. 17, no. 1, (Jan/Feb, 1993): 51.

11. Farley, *Personal Commitments,* 94.

12. Ibid., 106.

13. Handy, *The Age of Paradox,* 50.

14. Ibid., 51.

15. Ibid., 54–55. Although she does not use the language of *second-curve thinking,* Wallerstein makes a similar point about the importance of initiating change. "My sense is that by introducing change into their lives by reshaping the marriage tasks, these couples blocked crises that might have disrupted their relationship. . . . Instead of each person going outside of the relationship to seek new stimuli, they were able to refashion the marriage to fit their changed needs," *The Good Marriage,* 281.

16. Jacob Needleman, *Consciousness and Tradition* (New York: Crossroad Publishing Co., 1982), 7.

17. Handy, *The Age of Paradox,* 63.

18. Katharine Doob Sakenfeld, *Faithfulness in Action: Loyalty in Biblical Perspective* (Philadelphia: Fortress Press, 1985), 75–76.

19. Ibid., 137.

Chapter 2. When the Nest is Emptying

1. Rhodes, *Surviving Family Life,* 195.

2. Evelyn Millis Duvall and Brent C. Miller, *Marriage and Family Development* (New York: Harper & Row, 6th ed., 1985), 264.

3. Ibid., 288.

4. Sue Miller, *For Love* (New York: HarperCollins), 386. Judith Wallerstein makes this connection between leaving home and promising again. "At midlife the original task of marriage, separating from the families of origin and establishing new connections, must be solved anew. Now, however, the task is to separate from and make new connections with young adult children. . . . At this stage the issue is to let go of the marriage that was defined by children and to create in its place a new one in which the partners are once again focused on each other," *The Good Marriage,* 272.

5. Herbert Anderson and Susan B. W. Johnson, *Regarding Children: A New Respect for Childhood and Families* (Louisville, Ky.: Westminster John Knox Press, 1994), especially 29–47.

6. Donald S. Williamson, *The Intimacy Paradox: Personal Authority in the Family System* (New York: Guilford Press, 1991).

7. Daniel Day Williams, *The Spirit and the Forms of Love* (New York: Harper & Row, 1968). "It is not only that in committing oneself to another we take the risks of certain kinds of suffering. It is that we accept the inevitability of being conformed to the other. When we love, we enter a history in which suffering is one condition of the relationship. We are to be conformed to the need of another" (117).

8. Handy, *The Age of Paradox*, 88.

9. Wallerstein, *The Good Marriage*, 69.

10. *Book of Blessings* prepared by International Commission on English in the Liturgy (Collegeville, Minn.: The Liturgical Press, 1989). On one Sunday morning worship, in a congregation that each year honors those who have been married for more than 25 years, the pastor tabulated that 95 couples had been married a total of 3,909 years and had therefore greeted one another across the breakfast table approximately 1,407,240 times.

11. Farley, *Personal Commitments*, 13.

Chapter 3. When the Unexpected Occurs

1. David H. Olson, Candyce S. Russell, and Douglas H. Sprenkle, eds., *Circumplex Model: Systemic Assessment and Treatment of Families* (New York: Haworth Press, 1989), 12.

2. Frank S. Pittman III, *Turning Points: Treating Families in Transition and Crisis* (New York: W. W. Norton & Co., 1987), 70.

3. Shirley M. Smith, "Disaster: Family Disruption in the Wake of Natural Disaster," in Charles R. Figley and Hamilton I. McCubbin, eds., *Stress and the Family: Coping with Catastrophe*, vol. 2 (New York: Brunner/Mazel, 1983), 138.

4. Ibid., 186.

5. Ester R. Shapiro, *Grief as a Family Process: A Developmental Approach to Clinical Practice* (New York: Guilford Press, 1994), 186.

6. Froma Walsh and Monica McGoldrick, "Loss and the Family Life Cycle," in *Family Transitions: Continuity and Change over the Life Cycle*, ed. Celia Jaes Falicov (New York: Guilford Press, 1988), 321.

7. Judith Guest, *Ordinary People* (New York: Ballantine Books, 1976), 117–18.

8. Shapiro, *Grief as a Family Process*, 187.

9. Fredda Herz Brown, "The Impact of Death and Serious Illness on the Family Life Cycle," in Betty Carter and Monica McGoldrick, eds., *The Changing Family Life Cycle*, 2nd ed. (New York: Gardner Press, Inc., 1988), 467.

10. Norman L. Paul, "The Use of Empathy in the Resolution of Grief," *Perspectives in Biology and Medicine* (Autumn, 1967).

11. Nancy Gieseler Devor, "Pastoral Care of Infertile Couples," *Journal of Pastoral Care*, vol. 48, no. 4, (Winter, 1994): 355–60.

12. John S. Rolland, M.D., "Chronic Illness and the Family Life Cycle" in Carter and McGoldrick, *The Changing Family Life Cycle*, 435.

13. Patricia Voydanoff, "Unemployment: Family Strategies for Adaptation," in Figley and McCubbin, *Stress and the Family*, 91.

14. Pittman, *Turning Points*, 66.

Chapter 4. When Marriage Flounders

1. Karen Keyser, *When Love Dies: The Process of Marital Disaffection* (New York: Guilford Press, 1993).

2. Howard Markman, Scott Stanley, and Susan L. Blumberg, *Fighting for Your Marriage: Positive Steps for Preventing Divorce and Preserving a Lasting Love* (San Francisco: Jossey-Bass, Publishers, 1994).

3. Erik H. Erikson, *Identity and the Life Cycle,* vol. 1, no. 1, (New York: International Universities Press, Inc., 1959), 89.

4. Clifford Sager, *Marriage Contracts and Couple Therapy: Hidden Forces in Intimate Relationships* (Northvale, N.J.: Jason Aronson, Inc., 1994).

5. Harville Hendrix, *Getting the Love You Want: A Guide for Couples* (New York: Henry Holt & Company, 1988), xvii. For Hendrix, the unconscious expectation in selecting our marital partners is that they will magically provide a feeling of wholeness lost in our childhood. "You fell in love because your old brain had your partner confused with your parents! Your old brain believed that it had finally found the ideal candidate to make up for the psychological and emotional damage you experienced in childhood," ibid. We understand our emphasis on promising again to be a continuation of the work we need to do once we have identified our conscious expectations of marriage.

6. Sager, *Marriage Contracts,* 51.

7. Tom F. Driver, *The Magic of Ritual* (San Francisco: HarperCollins, 1991).

Chapter 5. When Marrying Again

1. We are particularly indebted to the work of Emily B. Visher and John S. Visher regarding second marriages and the families that are formed because of them. *Old Loyalties, New Ties: Therapeutic Strategies with Stepfamilies* (New York: Brunner/Mazel, 1988).

2. Evan Imber-Black and J. Roberts, *Rituals for our Times: Celebrating, Healing, and Changing Our Lives and Our Relationships* (New York: HarperCollins, 1992), 276–304.

3. Betty Carter and Monica McGoldrick, "Forming a Remarried Family," in Carter and McGoldrick, *The Changing Family Life Cycle,* 399–429.

4. Ibid., 410.

5. Herbert Anderson and Robert Cotton Fite, *Becoming Married* (Louisville, Ky.: Westminster/John Knox Press, 1993), 6.

6. Ibid., 37.

7. Virginia G. Clemente, "A Proposal for Preparation for Readiness for Remarriage after Divorce," in James J. Young, C.S.P., *Divorce Ministry and the Marriage Tribunal* (Rahway, N.J.: Paulist Press, 1982).

Chapter 6. Transformation in Marriage

1. Flora Slosson Wuellner, "Transformation: Our Fear, Our Longing," in *Weavings: A Journal of the Christian Spiritual Life,* vol. 6, no. 2 (March/April, 1991), 6–14.

2. Paul Watzlawick, John Weakland, and Richard Fisch, M.D., *Change:*

Principles of Problem Formation and Problem Resolution (New York: W. W. Norton & Co., 1974), 10–11. The emphasis on the change of change or second-order change corresponds with the growing awareness that adaptation, however necessary, is not enough. "Increasingly, the outcome of interest is adaptation, the ability of a family to recover from stress and crisis; however, this concept, like coping, is perceived by some researchers as not a definitive end product because families are always growing and changing and the serenity and stability synonymous with adaptation are not always functional for family members." Patrick C. McKenry and Sharon J. Price, "Families Coping with Problems and Change," in *Families and Change: Coping with Stressful Events,* eds. Patrick C. McKenry and Sharon J. Price (Thousand Oaks, Calif.: Sage, 1994), 16.

3. Rosemary Haughton, *The Transformation of Man* (Springfield, Ill.: Templegate Publishers, 1980), 244.

4. Ibid., 80.

5. Ibid., 72–73.

6. Beverly Roberts Gavanta, *From Darkness to Light: Aspects of Conversion in the New Testament* (Philadelphia: Fortress Press, 1986), 40.

7. Romney M. Moseley, *Becoming a Self Before God: Critical Transformations* (Nashville: Abingdon Press, 1991), 61.

8. Ibid., 119.

9. Ibid., 65.

10. Haughton, *The Transformation of Man,* 67.

11. Ibid., 68.

12. Nicholas Lash, *Easter in Ordinary: Reflections on Human Experience and the Knowledge of God* (Notre Dame, Ind.: University of Notre Dame Press, 1986), 194.

13. Ibid., 253.

14. Haughton, *The Transformation of Man,* 7.

15. Ibid., 81.

16. Ibid., 154.

17. Don S. Browning, *A Fundamental Practical Theology: Descriptive and Strategic Proposals* (Minneapolis: Fortress Press, 1991), 281.

18. Williamson, *The Intimacy Paradox,* 4.

19. Ted Peters, *God—The World's Future: Systematic Theology for a Postmodern Era* (Minneapolis: Fortress Press, 1992), 19.

20. Ibid., 135.

21. Handy, *The Age of Paradox,* 97.

22. Louis Janssens, "Norms and Priorities of a Love Ethic," *Louvain Studies 6* (1977). The application of the work of Janssens was first connected with family studies by Marie McCarthy, S.P., in her study titled "The Role of Mutuality in Family Structure and Relationships: A Critical Examination of Selected Options in Contemporary Theological Ethics," Ph.D. dissertation, University of Chicago, 1984. Subsequently, Janssens's emphasis on love as equal regard has become a major theme in the writings of Don and Carol Browning on the family. See especially "The Church and the Family Crisis: A New Love Ethic," in *The Christian Century,* vol. 108, no. 23, (August 7–14, 1991), 746–49.

23. David Tracy, *On Naming the Present: God, Hermeneutics, and the Church* (Maryknoll, N.Y.: Orbis Books, 1994). Tracy has contributed to understanding the relationship between love as equal regard and love as sacrifice by suggesting that, "authentic love is presented (in the New Testament) as pure gift and radical command," 99. Self-transcendence preserves both the drive of the self for authentic fulfillment and the need for self-discipline. This emphasis on balancing the drive for fulfillment and the need for authentic discipline is another way of understanding what we mean by *creative fidelity*.

24. Haughton, *The Transformation of Man,* 272.

25. Gabriel Marcel, "The Mystery of the Family," in *Homo Viator,* trans. by Emma Craufurd. (New York: Harper Torchbooks, 1962), 69.

26. Ibid., 72.